Praise for *The Barbie Chronicles*

"Whatever your position on the world's most persistent posable piece of plastic, you'll find much to intrigue you in this provocative collection that examines Barbie from all angles—with perspicacity and panache."

—Faye Moskowitz, author of *A Leak in the Heart*

"Equal parts celebration, confession, and investigation, *The Barbie Chronicles* takes shrewd measure of just how much we are what we buy."

—Albert Mobilio, winner of The National Book Critics Circle Award for Excellence in Reviewing

A Living Doll Turns **40**

THE BARBIE CHRONICLES

edited by

YONA ZELDIS McDONOUGH

A TOUCHSTONE BOOK
Published by SIMON & SCHUSTER

TOUCHSTONE
Rockefeller Center
1230 Avenue of the Americas
New York, NY 10020

Introduction and all introductions to essays copyright ©
1999 by Yona Zeldis McDonough.

All other copyright information may be found on page 233.

TOUCHSTONE and colophon are registered trademarks of
Simon & Schuster, Inc.

DESIGNED BY JUDITH STAGNITTO ABBATE

Manufactured in the United States of America

10 9 8 7 6 5 4 3 2 1

Library of Congress Cataloging-in-Publication Data

The Barbie chronicles / [edited by] Yona Zeldis
    McDonough.
        p.   cm.
    Includes bibliographical references and index.
    I. Barbie dolls—History.   I. McDonough, Yona Zeldis.
NK4894.3.B37B   1999
688.7'221—dc21   99-15725
                                              CIP

ISBN 0-684-86275-1

ACKNOWLEDGMENTS

I would like to thank the following people for their help and encouragement in assembling this volume: Kenneth E. Silver, Eric Copage, Eric Marcus, Diane Cardwell, Katharine Turok, Nancy Ramsey, Lisa Jackson, Sarah King, and the Art Department at Williams College, whose generosity made the publication of the pictures possible. Olivia Blumer at the Barney Karpfinger Agency deserves special mention for her clarity of purpose and direction. And an armload of thanks to my editor, Marah Stets, who gave this project her absolute all.

—YONA ZELDIS MCDONOUGH

CONTENTS

HAPPY BIRTHDAY TO YOU!

POSTMODERN MUSE

OUR DAUGHTERS, THEIR BARBIES

THE BARBIE CHRONICLES

INTRODUCTION

When I first sat down in the summer of 1997 to pen a piece about Barbie, I imagined writing a wry, affectionate defense of the sexy little doll who seemed to be getting so much bad press. Little did I know how Barbie had changed in the three decades since she and I had parted company. I didn't really understand the fantastic impact she had made on American culture during those years nor the maelstrom of controversy that her mere name seemed to elicit. But the publication of my essay on the back page of *The New York Times Magazine* filled me in quickly: Barbie had been busy all this time, what with her brand-new professions, newly reconfigured face, hair, and, yes, even body.

Ever since her 1959 debut, Barbie has been an amazingly popular doll. Created by Ruth and Elliot Handler in the late 1950s and named for their daughter, Barbara, Barbie has her origins in the German Lilli doll, a quasi-pornographic toy intended for men. The Handlers cleaned her up and toned her down before presenting her to the American market, but her inherent sexuality—so stunning in a world of baby dolls and little girl dolls—remained intact, just waiting for a generation of American children to discover her.

Discover and fall head over heels in love. Her phenomenal success in the intervening years has spawned enough Barbie dolls to populate a small planet, to say nothing of the ancillary characters—Skipper, Francie, Midge, Ken, Allan, and Kelly—that fill her world.

The girls who played with the very first Barbies are now grown, with Barbie-toting daughters of their own. But Barbie continues to exert a hold on their imaginations, as well as the imaginations of the boys who watched—envious, disdainful, titillated, curious—as their sisters, cousins, friends, and neighbors dressed, and undressed, their sexy, ever-so-adult-looking dolls.

Forty years after her debut, Barbie is big news and big business. Millions of dolls, clothes, accessories, and paraphernalia are bought and sold every year. There are Barbie conventions, fan clubs, Web sites, and scores of publications.

There is also, I soon discovered, a whole new literature of Barbie that emerged in the shadow of the consumer frenzy she created. She has inspired novelists and poets, commentators and journalists, and academics from a wide range of fields. No longer just a child's toy, Barbie has become an icon and a fetish—to some angelic, to others depraved. And as such, she serves as a kind of springboard for a whole range of cultural discourse, some philosophical and reflective, some lighthearted and appreciative, some furious and damning.

The Barbie Chronicles both grows out of and adds to the current conversation about Barbie. In it, I have included twenty essays and five poems written from varying intellectual perspectives as well as differing emotional ones. Some are original works commissioned specifically for this volume; others are reprinted from existing material. But whatever the take on Barbie is, it is never neutral.

Anna Quindlen proposes driving a stake through Barbie's plastic heart, while Melissa Hook remembers her as a conduit through which she could connect with her frosty and distant grandmother. For these writers, Barbie has a talismanic power, one that illuminates both the world without and the self within. Here then are stories that will, I hope, shed a little more light on the meaning of America's most beloved, most notorious piece of posable plastic.

$\mathcal{I}$n 1994, *cultural sociologist Steven Dubin was asked to join the creative team that produced* Art, Design and Barbie: The Evolution of a Cultural Icon, *organized by Exhibitions International. The show was to be composed of three sections: a history of dolls; a diaroma of various models of Barbie and friends since 1959, along with images of momentous events of the times; and a selection of artworks incorporating the doll. Dubin participated in the planning sessions and was commissioned to write one of the catalog essays, a critical examination of Barbie set against a broad sociohistorical backdrop.*

But when the essay was completed, executives from Mattel, which had contributed funding to the exhibition, were not happy with the result, and asked Dubin to delete certain material, such as a discussion of Earring Magic Ken in which that doll's homoerotic significance is explored. Also objectionable was a reference to the fact that Ruth Handler, Mattel's cofounder, had been indicted on multiple counts of fraud and conspiracy in 1974, although Handler herself was quite forthcoming about this in her 1994 memoir, Dream Doll.

While Dubin was willing to jettison some—although not all—of the material to which Mattel objected, the essay was ultimately pulled from the catalog. It appears here in full for the first time under the title "Who's That Girl? The World of Barbie Deconstructed."

WHO'S THAT GIRL?
THE WORLD OF BARBIE
DECONSTRUCTED

Steven C. Dubin

*A*ndy Warhol bequeathed fifteen minutes of fame to each of us. But few personalities transcend their brief moment in the spotlight. Except, of course, that pantheon of pop-culture icons we recognize by merely one name: Elvis and Marilyn, even the singer formerly known as Prince. Can there be any question that we must add Barbie to this illustrious roster?

Barbie (along with Mickey Mouse) is as close as we have to a global litmus test for being human: If you fail to recognize her, you're hardly of this world. That's why a trendy coffee bar in New York City's Chelsea district tags its bathroom doors with her and pal Ken, replacing the prosaic international symbols for female and male. Amazingly, Barbie is sold in 140 countries. And, according to *Smithsonian* magazine, if you queued up every one of the leggy dolls sold in its first thirty years—arrayed end to end from her lush tresses to her notoriously arched feet—you could circumnavigate the globe four times.

Two Barbies are sold each second, worldwide. That's right, *each* second. And the average American girl between the ages of three and ten owns ten of them. Her friends are legion: Barbie sales exceeded $2 billion in 1997, and Mattel, Incorporated, is the fourth-largest manufacturer of women's garments in the United States. (She's proportioned, incidentally, as a mannequin specifically designed to display fashions in the most flattering way.)

Since the fall of communism, little girls in Russia have abandoned the drab, bulkier dolls of local pedigree in favor of Barbie, the flashy Western newcomer, *if* their parents can spare a month's wages. And after several failed attempts to ignite the interest of Japanese girls—Mattel designers have even tried at times to "soften" their doll's appearance with more childlike features—Barbie finally appears to have staked a claim in one of the most xenophobic societies in the world. Barbie a dumb blond, as some argue? Think again!

*A*mericans love tales of humble beginnings. Horatio Alger heroes pull themselves up from the streets to the corporate board room. Farm boys learn by candlelight and ascend to the White House. Small-town girls board Greyhound buses to Hollywood, where they are discovered sitting on drugstore stools. Never mind that these are exceptions to the rule, and increasingly out of sync with contemporary American realities. We relish such myths, accounts of people making themselves over, giving birth to a more glamorous, successful, or powerful self.

Consider, then, the rather tawdry circumstances of Barbie's genesis. Ruth Handler's epiphany came in 1956 during a European sojourn. Handler (who founded Mattel with her husband, Elliot) was shopping with daughter Barbara when the girl discovered the *Bild* Lilli doll, a risqué novelty item derived from a popular cartoon strip. Lilli was designed for men. But Handler's recurrent thoughts about developing an adult doll for little girls—onto which they could project fantasies of themselves as mature young women, not just as future mothers tending to babies—were finally given physical form. In 1959, with a few modifications, Barbie was born.

The toy industry was a little sluggish to embrace her va-va-va-voom image, but Barbie quickly attracted an appreciative audience, in no small measure due to Mattel's savvy marketing—the Handlers brought aboard a merchandising wizard whose expertise was touted in Vance Packard's 1957 book, *The Hidden Persuaders*, and their advertising blitz on the *Mickey Mouse Club* turned toys into a year-round business.

Ken followed in 1961 (and yes, he is the namesake of the Handlers' other child). Barbie's prominent breasts are still the lightning rod for controversy; the quandary over Ken was what Mattel gingerly referred to as the "bulge" or the "bump." The corporate decision? Hapless Ken became a eunuch, distinctively embodying Gertrude Stein's dictum "there isn't any there there."

In her 1994 memoir, *Dream Doll*, Ruth Handler comes off as a no-nonsense, scrappy dame. A first-generation American born in 1916 of Polish-Jewish parents, she is clearly a true believer in the *Goldene Medina*, the golden land, the American Dream. During Handler's long entrepreneurial career, initiated in the prefeminist era, she reports that she was often the sole woman present at important business meetings. The company offered women previously unheard-of opportunities and responsibilities, and Handler prides herself that Mattel had a racially diverse workforce before it was an accepted practice. She sounds like a cross between Sinatra—she did it *her* way—and Leona Helmsley.

Counterbalancing our fascination with the triumph of people against the odds is our delight when they stumble. We love to dish the dirt, discover that our heroes have feet of clay. Coincidentally, both Helmsley and Handler faced what they felt were unfair criminal prosecutions. The 1974 charges against Barbie's mother were mail fraud, conspiracy, and making false statements about corporate earnings to the SEC. Handler pleaded nolo contendere, received a hefty fine, and was sentenced to probation and community service.

After Handler left Mattel, she developed Nearly Me, a breast prosthesis with a natural look and feel. A breast cancer survivor herself, Handler proclaims in her autobiography, "When I conceived Barbie, I believed it was important to a little girl's self-esteem to play with a doll that has breasts. Now I find it even more important to return that self-esteem to women who have lost theirs."

𝒫undits employ the term *zeitgeist* to describe the temper of the times, the "feel" of a particular era. How, then, might we characterize the late 1950s, the time of Barbie's birth, the height of the fabled "baby boom" generation?

Historians such as Philippe Aries have painstakingly documented that the prolonged childhood and adolescence commonplace today is a fairly recent historical development. In the past, most children could not be so indulged; economic necessity and a shorter life span dictated that they become workers and marriage partners at an early age.

Not so the children who were born into post–World War II America. A time of widespread optimism and economic growth—especially in contrast to the Great Depression of the 1930s and the sacrifices of the war years—more people savored a comfortable and rising standard of living than ever before. Suburbs blossomed and the middle class swelled into a new position of cultural dominance. The generally strong economy bolstered the nuclear family, with its duties neatly split by gender: men primarily handled the public sphere of work, women reigned over the private realm of home and hearth.

Revisionists have taught us two things about the 1950s. First, the families of *The Donna Reed Show, Leave It to Beaver,* and *Father Knows Best* may dominate our collective consciousness, but their ascendence in the 1950s was an anomaly. It turns out that the conditions which made them possible for many white Americans were only briefly in alignment. They stand out in stark contrast to the extended families that preceded them and the single-parent, "blended," and wide variety of alternative arrangements that predominate today.

Second, not all was well beneath the supposedly placid surface. A Cold War fueled a persistent anxiety and dictated both national and international policy making. Racial minorities, systematically excluded from sharing in the prosperity, began the push for greater inclusion through the emerging Civil Rights movement. Women, too, chafed under their restricted roles, a problem Betty Friedan momentously identified in her 1962 book, *The Feminine Mystique*, as "the problem that has no name." And some young people idolized "bad boys" like Marlon Brando and James Dean, perhaps even electing to join the counterculture of the period, the Beats.

Maverick filmmaker John Waters picked up many of these threads in *Hairspray*, where racial and generational conflict explodes and the clean-cut fans of singers from the Frankie Avalon mold face off against the supporters of a funkier, more uninhibited type of expression. Yet members of each group shared something important: They were part of a youth culture of unprecedented size, nurtured upon the electronic mass media, and wielding extraordinary purchasing power.

In other words, in the 1950s as never before, there were hordes of kids with money to spend. Smart manufacturers pitched their goods through television, radio—wherever they were likely to catch the eyes and ears of young people. Unlike the children of previous generations, these youngsters were more often consumers than they were producers. And few of them were liable to be content with old-fashioned baby dolls or facsimiles of stodgy adults when a swinging single like Barbie was offered to them instead.

*   *   *

$\mathcal{B}$irthdays can be great fun, a standard excuse to celebrate. But nationally syndicated columnist Anna Quindlen was not in a playful mood when Barbie turned thirty-five in 1994 [see "Barbie at 35," page 117]. Alternately suggesting that a silver stake be driven through the doll's heart or that several pieces of cake be urged upon her, Quindlen pointed an accusing finger:

> [L]ong before [supermodel] Kate [Moss] and Ultra Slim-fast came along, hanging over the lives of every little girl born in the second half of the twentieth century was the impossibly curvy shadow (40-18-32 in life-size terms) of Barbie. That preposterous physique, we learn as kids, is what a woman looks like with her clothes off.

Quindlen is not alone in expressing concern over messages regarding looks and self-worth. Best-selling authors Naomi Wolf and Susan Faludi argue that women are tyrannized by cultural ideals which calibrate their importance by their appearance more than by their accomplishments, unlike men. Significantly, however, neither of these writers cite Barbie in the arsenal of symbolic weapons they inventory.

Quindlen indirectly unites Barbie with other American bugaboos commonly cited as the wellspring of serious contemporary social problems, such as television and pornography. Now that's a mighty burden to shoulder, especially when you're made of plastic. For convenience's sake, many of us prefer to attribute human behavior to lone causes rather than consider the spectrum of factors that contribute to all our values and behaviors: Increased sex and violence in the media lead directly to their escalation in the real world, so the simple argument goes. Likewise, wherever pornography is made available, sexual aggression toward women increases. And playing with Barbie causes girls to emulate her lean yet buxom figure, as well as imparts materialistic values.

Intriguing speculation, yes. But such pronouncements are not backed up by hard data. Human behavior is too complex to be reduced to single origins. That's what's both fascinating and frustrating about studying people's conduct: They constantly confound your predictions and defy your best theories—unless you're in the realm of fantasy, that is, as with the 1993 film *Addams Family Values.* Joan Cusack plays Debbie, a "black widow" who preys on wealthy bachelors. In the movie's penultimate scene, she presents a slide show of her life, demonstrating how someone coming from a white picket–fence background becomes a ruthless killer: "My parents, Sharon and Dave. Generous, doting; or were they? All I ever wanted was a Ballerina Barbie. In her pretty pink tutu. My birthday [slide]. I was ten. And do you know what they got me? *Malibu* Barbie. . . . That's not what I wanted. That's not who I was." Next we see flames engulf her childhood home, projected behind the monster she's become. The comic impact is undeniable, but seldom are explanations so precise or effects so direct in real life.

Quindlen cited two studies reporting that teenaged girls have seriously distorted body images as "evidence" of Barbie's negative repercussions. In the first, 90 percent of white girls were discontent with their bodies, while 70 percent of black girls were satisfied with their weight. In another report, 83 percent of girls polled felt they needed to lose weight, even though 62 percent were in fact within normal limits. There is no denying that eating disorders such as anorexia nervosa and bulimia represent the malaise of women in the late twentieth century much like hysteria symbolized the Victorian age. Each disturbance symbolically enacts the anxieties of its particular time. But to single out Barbie as *the* cause of such distress misses the important point that this doll reflects the times as well as influences them. It is as much effect as cause.

Artist Portia Munson senses the complexity and magnitude of the issue in her *Pink Project* (1994), a staggering installation of hundreds of pink items on a large table: row upon obsessive row of combs, brushes, toys, dollies, accessories. Barbie appears only briefly in this frightful cache; she is a tiny element in this avalanche of products available to young girls. Munson's work conjures up visions of a vast, bubbling, primordial plastic ooze from which Barbie, as well as our notions of femininity, emerge.

Not surprisingly, Barbie's influence *is* unequivocally direct in a few instances. Take the character in Barbara Kingsolver's novel *Pigs in Heaven* who legally changes her name to "Barbie TM" and fabricates her Barbie-inspired ensembles from whatever she can glean from thrift shops. But as is often the case, truth is stranger than fiction. The most extreme example is Cindy Jackson, who has embraced Barbie as a template for her own body as well as for her personality: After spending more than $100,000 on over twenty surgical procedures, on an as-yet incomplete transformative project, she's become a bona fide living doll. Intelligent enough to be a member of Mensa (the association for those with high IQs), she nonetheless seems to be someone grasping for an identity.

As Jackson described her transformation on *The Jerry Springer Show,* "It was just a nice face. [But] I didn't want to be nice. I wanted to be glamorous." A frequent talk-show guest, she elaborated to Jenny Jones, "I didn't want to be a farmer's wife [she grew up in rural Ohio]. I didn't want to work in the factory." So Jackson fled to England, where she shed her dowdy self and her past. How does she view herself now? On *Dateline NBC* she declared, "I don't want to be a bimbo, but I don't mind looking like one."

The probability of a little girl following in Cindy Jackson's footsteps must equal the odds of a meteor striking a specific spot on the earth's crust. Be that as it may, many adults project a variety of fears onto their children's playthings. A Mommy-to-Be doll upset some Omaha residents in 1992, alarmed that a pregnant doll might "traumatize" a young child. Mattel's Growing-Up Skipper garnered considerable media attention and generated similar concerns in 1975; a thrust of her arm backward, and she magically grew breasts. Tongues clucked over its appropriateness. And M. G. Lord reports that Mattel's anatomically correct Baby Brother Tenderlove drew cheers from some that same year, but not in Louisville, Kentucky: Irate women besieged a toy store, leaving castrated dolls in their wake.

While "negative" messages or role models regarding sexuality are a primary concern, other toys provoke distress over supposedly inciting violence (Teenage Mutant Ninja Turtles and Power Rangers), or even breeding insensitivity and causing desensitization to others' pain (Disney withdrew its Steve the Tramp doll in 1990 after protestors decried its uncompassionate portrayal of the homeless). And in one of the most notable controversies, critics assailed Mattel's Teen Talk Barbie in 1992 when one of the 270 possible sayings she was programmed to repeat was reported to be "math class is tough." No less a group than the august American Association of University Women jumped into the fray. Mattel ultimately capitulated, altering the computer chip and offering the AAUW an advisory role in planning future models. (The 1995 product line introduced Teacher Barbie, putting the doll on the other side of the blackboard.)

In all these instances, adults stepped in to protect children from what they as adults perceived to be harmful. But a major fallacy underlies such responses: It's folly to presume that kids see and understand Barbie or any other toy exactly the way their parents do. This betrays the arrogance of age that underestimates the degree to which children *actively* incorporate their toys into their personal world of play. To put it simply, kids constantly manipulate playthings as they uniquely see fit. This is vividly conveyed in an installment of the comic strip *Phoebe and the Pigeon People:* Parents buy their five-year-old daughter a tool kit instead of a Barbie to counteract gender-role stereotyping. You overhear the child at play, animating the implements. Holding a hammer in one hand, she implores, "Barbie, would you go to the prom with me?" The girl coquettishly responds through a wrench, "Oh, Ken, I'd love to!"

Obviously, children can derail the best intentions of their parents. A real example: In 1991, Cathy Meredig, a former industrial engineer who started her own company, introduced the Happy to Be Me doll, designed to more accurately reflect the body proportions of typical women. Consumers ignored it, making it a notable failure in the marketplace. But to be fair, it's impossible to parse out to what extent this can be attributed to the design, or to the probability that most newcomers will lose when they step up to compete against huge corporations. The bottom line for concerned parents: Children filter their experiences through the values and behaviors they are taught by their elders. It's unlikely that a doll will cause serious fissures in a youngster's core once his or her parents lay down a strong foundation.

Ask anyone to reminisce about Barbie, and one sort of story constantly emerges: Children routinely modify her appearance. The art critic for the *Kansas City Star* reports that her brother drew nipples on her Barbies (possibly the most common alteration) and culled stray hairs from a hairbrush to provide Barbie with pasted-on pubic hair. Excuse the pun, but she becomes plastic in children's hands. They turn Barbie into what *they* want her to be. Kids mutilate her (like the narrator of A. M. Homes's story "A Real Doll" does), create tableaus with her and other characters, and undress, redress, and cross-dress her (typically switching wardrobes with Ken or G.I. Joe). Barbara Kingsolver's young character Turtle even has a "Rastafarian Barbie," created by accident, not design. Her mother explains, "This one isn't on the market. It's been rolling under the bed too long with the dust bunnies."

Barbie is the most protean of characters, not only because of the variety of roles Mattel has developed for her over the years—from student teacher to stewardess to nurse, astronaut, doctor, soldier in Operation Desert Storm, and even a candidate for president in 1992—but because of the profusion of uses, guises, and situations her enthusiasts develop for her. One gay man recalls that Barbie and Ken satisfied some of his questions about gender differences, but raised many more. A straight man reports that he feigned interest in Barbie several times to get closer to girls with whom he was interested in developing relationships. His play unintentionally helped him define a career: He went to design school, and now incorporates dolls into his artistic work. One lesbian professes to have had no interest in Barbie, ever. Another considers the Barbie Boutique at FAO Schwarz the ultimate site for a "dream date."

Barbie is nothing if not accommodating. Within limits, however. *Smithsonian* magazine describes Mattel's Barbie Exposure Gauge, a headless doll marked across the chest and rump with a blue line. Each new outfit is fitted against this standard, and should any blue be revealed, it is nixed. For all the accusations directed at Barbie for having a slatternly appearance, in actuality it's as if she's eternally stuck in Catholic school, perpetually kneeling before nuns who check the length of her hemline.

A collector in Montclair, New Jersey, who has turned her hobby into a business, sums up her feelings by explaining, "I played with Barbie as well as a lot of other dolls as a child—Betsy McCall, Tiny Tears—and I certainly didn't think I was going to be Betsy McCall when I grew up. A lot of women come into my store and say '*I* wasn't allowed to play with Barbie,' or '*I* won't allow my daughter to play with Barbie.' And it's just so silly. It's just a doll and it's just a fantasy. You make the situation. No matter which doll it is you play with as a child, *you* make up the idea. The doll doesn't make the idea."

In a classic essay, Walter Benjamin described his elation when he unpacked his beloved books: "O bliss of the collector," he exclaims toward the finale, "bliss of the man of leisure!" Benjamin wrote these words in 1931, an Eastern European Jew wary of the rise of Nazism. His passion loses none of its intensity over the years. Through his possessions he constructs a fresh order; he is omniscient and omnipotent in this realm, his books the building blocks of a new reality.

And who collects today? Those like Benjamin, of course, connoisseurs of fine bindings and objets d'art. And most children, too, cherishing commonplace objects such as shells, rocks, stamps, butterflies; practically anything can become personally engrossing. In between these poles are adults whose interest may also alight upon the most mundane things. Toys, matchbooks, bells, tea pots, salt and pepper shakers, lunch boxes—even carnivorous plants trigger something within certain people that leads them to hoard. In every case, regardless of the collector's age, resources, celebrity, or lack thereof, these people are in control of a world of their own invention.

One collector offers a cockamamie theory in *The Passionate Collector:* "I think the collecting spirit in human beings was slowly built up by natural selection. For hundreds of thousands of years survival depended upon gathering, accumulating and eventually storing for the winter or lean times. A hundred or so generations won't wipe out an ancient instinct."

We are confident that traits such as eye and hair color are passed through the generations. The gene for stockpiling, however, has not been isolated. In fact, the numerous instances when collectors postpone buying a good, warm coat in favor of purchasing *just one more item* attests to the possibility that this is a *non*adaptable behavior in some respects.

Psychoanalyst Werner Muensterberger has a different approach. He argues that collectors use objects to fend off feelings of helplessness, erecting a psychological dike to keep from being flooded with such anxious emotions. Think of this as Linus's security blanket writ large. One's selection of materials will likely be entwined with personal history: a Scottie dog you loved as a child, a television or comic book hero, or perhaps a doll. Whatever the target, collectors savor the hunt as much as displaying the spoils, and they relish seeing the repetition of the same basic form—such as row upon row of swizzle sticks or salt and pepper shakers—congruity alongside variation. Your family may not have always been there for you, but you can make sure your Barbies, Kens, and Skippers will be.

A vast network of Barbie collectors has sprung up: nourished by the support of like-minded cohorts in local Barbie clubs;

linked through newsletters, dealers' inventory lists, and the glossy bimonthly *Barbie Bazaar;* their persistent hunger at least temporarily satisfied by attending the numerous doll shows around the country. That hunger can gnaw at collectors. If they fixate upon a particular item they do not have, it's like the dull ache of a slowly rotting tooth. They *have* to have it, no matter what.

Listen to a woman describe her dogged search for the top hat from Ken's Here Comes the Groom: "For ten years I chased this outfit; I didn't care how I was getting this hat. Once I bid it up to $1,300 at an auction. There were so many horror stories. I would just miss it." After she recently secured it (to her, a bargain at $250), she "just stared at it. I couldn't believe I really had it." Before her zeal cooled, she found a new obsession: a tiny painting from a Barbie backdrop called Modern Art. Tellingly, she confessed, "Actually I like not having this painting. Because there's really nothing else for me to look for."

Try to imagine, then, the collector's ultimate nightmare: Your collection is stolen or destroyed. San Diego resident Glen Offield confronted the unthinkable in 1992. What happened sounds like the invention of a tabloid newspaper writer with a wicked imagination, yet it's all true: his million-dollar Barbie collection was stolen and held hostage by the kingpin of a drug and gay-pornography ring. Among the five thousand dolls were some one-of-a-kind prototypes. The "kidnapper" stashed the goods in self-storage, then tried to cover his tracks by torching the house where the collection originated. His goal: unload the booty on some rich Japanese in order to revitalize his failing finances.

Needless to say, Offield was devastated. He beseeched readers of the *Los Angeles Times,* "They meant everything to me. I could do without eating. I don't know if I can live without them." He eventually recovered his treasure, but only after the death of the perpetrator from an overdose.

Barbie collectors have invented a parallel universe, just as other aficionados of popular culture like Trekkies have done.

They turn over parts of their homes to Barbie, in extreme cases smudging the line between sideline and vocation, along the lines of Pee-Wee Herman and his fabled playhouse. Sometimes collectors re-create full-sized outfits for themselves (and even coax spouses and children to dress up), and they generally fine-tune their senses so they can accurately distinguish, say, a #1 from a #3 model Barbie by touch, sight, or smell, even across a crowded room. Especially if it's filled with other collectors on high alert for the same things.

Their interests are typically specialized: They collect a specific model (Barbie, but not Midge), a style (bubble cuts), or a type of fashion (glamour). Even so, their shared interest in this play world links together widely disparate people who would otherwise probably not cross paths.

Barbie collectors are both female and male, and many of the men are gay. It is commonplace to hear them describe the pursuit of their hobby as a second "coming out": First they disclose their sexuality. They later profess their love for Barbie. Both processes occur in stages, as the person becomes more and more comfortable with important changes in his identity. In both instances, friends and acquaintances may pass knowing glances well in advance of the formal announcement. "I'm buying these for my nieces," declares a man who just happens to know the name of every model and ensemble. Yeah, sure.

Many gay men report playing with Barbie. Or wishing to. In *Queer in America*, activist/journalist Michelangelo Signorile ruefully recalls that when his father discovered him and his five-year-old female cousin playing with Barbie together, he was forbidden to continue. "Only sissies play with dolls," his father proclaimed, and that was the end of that in their traditional Italian household.

The sentiments of the elder Signorile are partially backed up by the findings of psychiatrist Richard Green in *The "Sissy Boy Syndrome" and the Development of Homosexuality*. Green examined a number of measures that he argues distinguish feminine boys from masculine ones. One of his bar graphs is quite possibly the only such instance where Barbie's name is invoked in a scientific tome: "FIGURE 1.5 Extent of son's interest in female-type dolls (Barbie): parent report."

The results? *All* the "feminine boys" played with Barbie; for nearly 20 percent of them, she was their favorite toy. Over half the comparison group never played with Barbie, and she was the favorite toy for none of them. But note: four out of ten of the so-called masculine boys played with Barbie occasionally, underscoring the overlap between allegedly distinct categories. Lurking in the shadows of the life stories of untold numbers of outwardly straight men may be tales of hours of engrossing play with a certain blonde bombshell (or any of her ethnic counterparts).

According to Green, many of the children in the "sissy boy" group become homosexual in adulthood. Do we fault Barbie, just as the psychiatric establishment once held overprotective mothers responsible in the past? Hardly. Barbie no more "causes" homosexuality than she turns girls into materialistic monsters. She does, however, strike very deep chords in many, many children.

To the ranks of terrorist organizations now add the Barbie Liberation Organization. An insidious movement, its members are dedicated to striking fear into all those who support the John Wayne school of gender, who celebrate when "men were men" and "little ladies" awaited their attention and aid.

The group's first offensive was launched during the 1993 Christmas season. Reminiscent of the radical personality conversions in the classic 1956 sci-fi flick *Invasion of the Body Snatchers*, the BLO kidnapped Teen Talk Barbies and Talking Duke G.I. Joe dolls off store shelves, surgically switched their voice boxes, and then returned them, to the astonishment of unsuspecting customers. All might seem well on the surface, but once the dolls opened their mouths, they were clearly aberrations: dainty girls shouting "Eat lead, Cobra!" and butch guys proposing "Let's go shopping!"

A group of performance artists in New York City's East Village first claimed responsibility, and admitted to altering three hundred dolls. They were partially motivated, they insisted, by Barbie's infamous "math class is tough" gaffe the preceding year. According to a spokesperson whose identity was concealed on *Dateline NBC,* the BLO doubled its goal in 1994 from a California base of operations. They were committed to disrupting "teaching young girls to be passive, vacuous, and to shop."

BLO members have taken the temperature of the body politic and devised their own radical cure for what they feel ails it. As a society, we are experiencing what Marjorie Garber has labeled a "categorical crisis" in *Vested Interests,* her encyclopedic study of transvestism. Perhaps more than ever before, people are challenging taken-for-granted assumptions about masculinity and femininity.

Just think back over the list of recent movies featuring performers in drag. A sample: *Paris Is Burning; The Crying Game; Mrs. Doubtfire; The Adventures of Priscilla, Queen of the Desert; The Ballad of Little Jo; To Wong Foo, Thanks for Everything, Julie Newmar; Ed Wood; Just Like a Woman.* And don't forget "Pat," the exceptionally ambiguous creature on *Saturday Night Live.* Were "The Duke" still alive, he would doubtless be appalled.

Dolls lend themselves to this type of "deep play," anthropologist Clifford Geertz's term for activities where much more is at stake symbolically than is immediately apparent, as in, for example, a Balinese cockfight, where social status and identity enter the ring as well as the wish for a good return on a wager. Some dolls have sexual ambivalence or small blows against the gender empire built in. Shindana's 1970 Flip Wilson doll is a fine example. On the obverse side, the comedian appears as a man. Reverse, he is the sassy, bewigged character Geraldine. Pull its string and you hear a version of Wilson's familiar shtick, "The devil made me buy this dress!"

Still other dolls are also culturally subversive and socially revealing, such as topsy-turvy dolls, with a black face on one end, a white face on the other. Some people have suggested that these date back to slavery, when black children would remain alert to flip to the black side when whites were present. They were indisputably popular during the Jim Crow era of segregation in the late nineteenth and into the twentieth centuries, where they commonly featured both a black servant and a white mistress. Here the linkage of the torsos trenchantly exposed the interdependence of the two races. The Day-to-Night Barbie performs a somewhat similar switch-a-roo, the contemporary gal who does it all: turn her pink business suit inside out and she's wearing a stunning evening dress.

BLO supporters are not the only ones to sense the potential to use Barbie and her extended circle to comment upon society. Some unidentified guerrilla quick-change artist is probably responsible for a cross-dressed Ken that was sold in Tampa in 1990 ("So easy to dress!" the box announces). Mattel cited product tampering instead of a production error.

Although Mattel would probably recoil from the notion, it would seem that the company itself has been slowly blending a gay sensibility into certain of its products. In 1993, Mattel introduced Earring Magic Ken, replete with pierced ear, lavender mesh shirt, and faux-leather vest. He also sports what resembles a doll-sized cock ring around his neck. Long disappeared from most stores, it is still sold on Christopher Street, New York City's major gay thoroughfare. Or examine the mid-1990s City Cowboy ensemble, part of the Cool Times fashion series: black leather vest, stonewashed blue jeans, and black cowboy hat and boots. Fully outfitted, Ken looks like a hybrid of two members of the Village People. He would fit comfortably into any of the country's gay ghettos.

It is not easy to pigeonhole Mattel's relationship with the gay community. Or, for that matter, other minority constituencies. For example, in 1994, Mattel refused permission to the gay-oriented *Genre* magazine to use two Ken dolls to illustrate an article on first dates. The editors subsequently whited out the figures, conspicuously leaving only their outlines. On the other hand, Barbie's had black friends since the late sixties; she herself has come in a rainbow of hues since 1980. And Shindana Toys, a black-owned company set up in South Central Los Angeles after the Watts riots, was quietly mentored by Mattel, which offered invaluable support and business know-how. The Flip Wilson doll they produced bears the name of Operation Bootstrap, Inc., a community-based jobs program under which it was started.

Ken has stood loyally, patiently at Barbie's side for well over thirty years. Supposedly boyfriend and girlfriend, it's not exactly clear if the two ever married, even though they have been outfitted twice with the appropriate clothes. Could Ken have a secret that explains their puzzling relationship? Company policy would appear to be "Don't ask, don't tell," while Ken has been leaving behind some broad hints lately—dropping his hairpins, in gay parlance.

$\mathcal{B}$arbie has become an ummistakable reference point in our world. An irreverent birthday card asks, "Didn't you play with Barbie before there was a Ken?" She has seeped into our everyday lives, hawking products ranging from her own exercise video to adult women's pajamas, made from the same material designer Nicole Miller used to outfit Barbie. The cost? $298.

Or stroll through New York's East Village near Tompkins Square Park and you'll likely notice a small shop where diabolic experiences have befallen our heroine: It sells crucified Barbies, Barbies strung up in S&M attire, and Barbie trophies, where the doll has been cut in half at the waist, sheathed in fur and fitted with antlers, and then mounted like a hunting trophy. Moreover, the media regularly reports cheeky transmutations like Trailer Trash Barbie or Big Dyke Barbie being offered for sale, while similar audacious ideas and proposals proliferate on the Internet as well.

Barbie has become a mother lode of imagery for artists to mine. At least two of them have hurtled her down a stairway—naked, no less—à la Marcel Duchamp's cubist masterpiece *Nude Descending a Staircase* (1911–12). Other artists have insinuated Barbie into the desolate urban cityscapes of Edward Hopper, recast her as Edouard Manet's scandalous *Olympia* (1863) or Botticelli's Venus (from *The Birth of Venus,* c. 1482), pickled and mummified her, even pounded nails into her torso like an African fetish. One of the most compelling reworkings is that of Dean Brown, who transformed Barbie into the Venus de Milo. The work is startling *not* because her arms were amputated in the process—it derives its power from the fact that the artist provides her with a navel, thus endowing her with a sense of mortality.

Additional creative souls have used her to explore the "darker side" of contemporary gender relations, most notably Todd Haynes, whose celebrated 1987 movie *Superstar* used Barbie to portray the late Karen Carpenter, a victim of anorexia nervosa. Haynes and cowriter Cynthia Schneider skillfully penetrate the sunny facade of suburban Downey, California, revealing the cloying, dysfunctional dynamics of family life from a doll's-eye view. Withdrawn from public showings because of pressure by the Carpenter family and A&M Records, the film is a confirmed cult classic. In certain circles, a good index of how hip you are is whether you've caught a clandestine screening.

People typically adore Barbie or hate her. There's scant middle ground: Islamic fundamentalists in Kuwait even issued a fatwa against her in 1995, banning this Western "she-devil" with polished nails and short skirts. But regardless of your personal position, it's hard to deny that she's secured a significant place in the history of the late twentieth century. Generations from now, lucky archaeologists may stumble upon a cache of Barbie dolls and wardrobes, jammed with outfits carefully squirreled away by fervent collectors. Such a stockpile of plastic and synthetic fibers will undoubtedly outlast many animal and plant species. The scientists will likely be somewhat baffled by the peculiar body proportions yet awed by the ubiquitous pink, un-like anything they've ever seen. And if they're truly fortunate, they'll also uncover Andy Warhol's perky portrait of Barbie. Earnestly, forthrightly confronting her viewers, she reigns as the queen of consumer culture.

*L*ooking back at the decade of Barbie's birth—the straitlaced, sex-shy 1950s—it would be easy to think that Barbie represented a freakish aberration on an otherwise staid, pin-striped path. Not so at all, says Stephanie Coontz. In fact, the original, 1959 Barbie is nothing less than the logical, natural embodiment of her cultural moment. Her compelling and provocative sexual schism—body of a siren, persona of a cheerleader—accurately reflected the many contradictions of the time.

GOLDEN OLDIE:
BARBIE IN THE 1950s

Stephanie Coontz

How could a popular culture that doted on Gidget, Tammy, June Cleaver, Princess and Kitten (the two daughters in *Father Knows Best*), Donna Reed, and the Nelson family embrace Barbie, a doll who obviously appealed to little girls' fantasies about sexuality and whose explicit if implausible anatomy initially horrified most parents?[1] The real question is how could it not?

The marketability of toys like Barbie and of the real-life sex goddesses of the era (whose anatomical measurements were scarcely less incredible) was a logical, though ironic, extension of 1950s gender roles, marital norms, and consumerist values. Marilyn Monroe, Jayne Mansfield, Anita Ekberg, and Barbie might not have looked much like Debbie Reynolds or Sandra Dee, but they no more represented a challenge to conventional sexual mores than did those perky teen icons. Indeed, an explicit theme in 1950s pop culture was that both types of woman wanted the same thing in the end. Heroines such as Gidget envied their sexy rivals and tried to expand their busts; the celluloid sex goddesses never sought social or even sexual equality, but simply used their different endowments to land a husband.

The distance between the girl next door in the suburbs and the bombshell in the downtown apartment was never very far, either on-screen or off. If Ozzie and Harriet, the real-life couple whose family played an idealized version of itself on television, had had a daughter, she might very well have become a real-life Barbie, without ever rebelling against either her parents or the sponsors of their show. Consider what happens when we insert a fictional daughter into the actual documented history of the Nelson family.

As the youngest child in America's most popular family, Barbie's adorable lisp and darling little dresses would have enchanted viewers. For all her sprightly innocence, Barbie would soon have realized that a youthful version of the classic pinup pose—arms akimbo, one hip to the side, a pretty pout, and a well-placed look of hair in the eyes, for example—was almost guaranteed to reduce both family and viewers to putty. As she developed that sexy figure, parents and makeup artists would have taught Barbie how to choose clothes that revealed her narrow waist and impressive bust without seeming cheap. That, of course, was the tightrope that all "good girls" of the period aspired to traverse successfully.

Offstage, Barbie would have discovered a slightly more racy version of the tightrope act as she leafed through photos of her parents' life before the sitcom, when her mom was a sultry, platinum-blond nightclub singer. She would also have overheard the off-color jokes that her mother, the former Harriet Hilliard, still liked to tell over cocktails after a day's filming. Friends from the 1940s would have reminisced—when the guys weren't around, of course—about the days when they had worked beside men in the war industries or the nights they had painted the town with soldiers or sailors on leave. Clearly, it was possible to have a little fun before settling down into domesticity. Sometimes, Barbie gathered from her own family history, a girl who did so might even make a better catch than a girl who played only by the official rules of the game.

Besides, as part of the showbiz community, Barbie would have known how often those rules were broken behind the scenes. She wouldn't have realized that Sandra Dee, like Miss America 1958, had been an incest victim, but she would have learned that many of Dee's male costars were actually gay. She'd have heard the gossip about the sexual entanglements of the cast of *Leave It to Beaver* and the alcoholism of Robert Young, star of *Father Knows Best.* Then, of course, there was the well-publicized marriage of her twenty-three-year-old brother Rick, and the unpublicized—at the time—fact that his seventeen-year-old bride was three months pregnant at the wedding. How could an observant younger sister have missed knowing that their dad got the hospital to change the birth certificate and place the baby in an incubator so people would think she was premature?[2]

Such subterfuges probably wouldn't have estranged Barbie from parents who so clearly doted on her—and who introduced her to such well-connected people—but it might have helped justify some sneaking around behind her folks' backs. And it would certainly have reinforced the lesson that girls can break the rules, so long as they play their cards right and don't directly challenge male prerogatives. With all the role models in her family, Barbie would have played her cards exceptionally well. And despite periodic bouts of worry or disapproval, her parents would ultimately have been as proud of her as they were of Ricky.

$\mathcal{C}$lose examination of 1950s cultural trends supports the point of my little exercise in historical imagination: The appearance of Barbie (and her real-life successors, Helen Gurley Brown and those *Cosmo* girls) represented no break with mainstream sexual and gender norms. It was a logical consequence of postwar social evolution, a product of the same forces that produced the girl-next-door movies and the staid marriages of the sitcoms even as they also sent women to work in record numbers and paved the way for a recreational sexuality increasingly separated from reproductive constraints.

The 1940s set in motion rearrangements of gender roles that accelerated in the 1950s despite a massive cultural pretense to the contrary. Between 1940 and 1945, the female labor force grew by more than 50 percent, from 11,970,000 to 18,610,000. For the first time, many women did "men's work"—and had a taste of male economic independence. Soldiers, women workers, and migrants to the cities gained freedom from parental supervision and experimented with new sexual behavior. Compared to couples who wed in earlier decades, researchers found, college-educated couples who married in the early 1940s were more knowledgeable about sex, reported greater sexual satisfaction, and felt that sex was a more important arena of life.[3]

After the war, a sharp drop in the average age at which people were marrying, a resurgent ideology of domesticity, and a conservative political revival obscured the continuing transformation of women's economic and reproductive roles without reversing it. Despite highly publicized campaigns to rejuvenate women's homemaker role (including institution of what we now know as the "marriage penalty" tax for working couples, which increased taxes on dual-income couples specifically to encourage male-breadwinner families), most women did not permanently leave their jobs, but were simply downgraded to "women's work" after the war. By the early 1950s, more women were working outside the home than during the height of the war effort, and married women with school-age children were the fastest growing segment of the labor force. Young women certainly wanted to get married, but they also coveted the fun that a working "girl" might have before she settled down.[4]

Postwar idealization of the housewife and stay-at-home mother, moreover, coexisted with some very different themes.

Many business leaders and policymakers argued that women were needed in the workforce to answer the challenge of Communist Russia. While TV painted a rosy picture of housewifely bliss, magazine articles gave a different message, lauding marriage as the ultimate measure of a woman but also showing glamorous pictures of successful career women or reporting on the frustrations, boredom, and isolation faced by young mothers. At the same time, the mass media urged men to get more involved in family life, and the failure of real-life husbands to be as competent fathers as Ozzie Nelson and Ward Cleaver frustrated many wives and daughters.[5]

New expectations and disappointments were also created by the expansion of education in postwar America. Even conservative social scientists of the day, despite their complacency about 1950s social arrangements, noted the contradictions here. As sociologist John Seeley wrote in 1956, "The girl who in ten years will be rinsing diapers competes in the trigonometry class with the boy who will be an engineer—and often gets higher marks." Margaret Mead, more critical of the disparity, noted that society "appears to throw its doors wide open to women, but translates her every step towards success as having been damaging—to her own chances of marriage, and to the men whom she passes on the road."[6]

The prospect of motherhood evoked ambivalence for many women, given the recurring theme of 1950s social science and popular culture that almost all of society's ills could be blamed on rejecting, overprotective, domineering, emasculating, or even just "overaffectionate" mothers. Only a few women were as explicit as one who told interviewers at the time, "I sure don't want Betty to turn out to be a housewife like myself." But many encouraged their girls to wait longer than they had themselves before getting married. Such mothers were ready to buy their daughters some toys other than the little baby dolls designed to awaken girls' maternal urges. Barbie would probably not have been their first choice, but they were open to *some* alternative to products encouraging early marriages and childbirth.[7]

Even those housewives who embraced their role most ardently sometimes produced more complicated reactions in their daughters. Ilene Philipson suggests that many 1950s mothers overinvested in child rearing to give purpose to their lives, with the ironic twist that they became unable to distinguish their children's needs from their own. For boys, this created the narcissistic expectation that women existed to shore up their inflated sense of self-importance. For girls, the narcissism thus engendered could produce a preoccupation with sexual attractiveness, while simultaneously leading them to identify with a resentment that their mothers hardly acknowledged even to themselves. Such girls were easily bored by the sexless baby dolls and play kitchens that were their typical birthday presents.[8]

Although many girls responded to their contradictory emotions and experiences by resisting assignment to cheerful domesticity, almost invariably they rebelled through their relations with men rather than through assertion of their self-sufficiency. Some attached themselves to disaffected male subcultures, such as the beatniks or the teen outlaws celebrated in song and movies. Others deliberately cultivated a "bad girl" image.[9] But the path of least resistance was to expand preexisting tendencies in sexual mores and gender roles to accommodate more female initiative (or at least behind-the-scenes manipulation) in sexual expression and consumerist individualism without challenging the fundamental allocation of power and resources between the sexes. This was a path that led directly to the popularity of Barbie.

Contemporary sociologist Talcott Parsons noted that there were two ways to resolve "the widespread ambivalence among women toward the role of motherhood" without threatening the existing sexual division of labor. One was for women to work in socially approved community activities and to expand the companionate nature of marriage. Another, in Parsons's view less desirable but still socially conservative, was to focus on glamour and sex appeal. As Parsons recognized, women could seek power and fulfillment in sexual display without threatening men's occupational supremacy or breadwinning prestige. Despite the implicit discontent this choice reflected, it did not undermine the segregation of sex roles.[10]

Nor did it represent a challenge to existing sexual mores. Despite the surface prudery of the period, sexuality already permeated the culture. As one woman later recalled, there were "Stop-Go lights flashing everywhere we looked. Sex, its magic spell everywhere, was accompanied by the stern warning: Don't do it." But invitations to jaywalk were also everywhere. Girls wore makeup, lipstick, and training bras well before puberty; they went on prom dates in middle school and were "going steady" by their freshman year of high school. Many teenagers were "doing it" from a fairly early age, as attested to by both the early age of marrying couples and the fact that the rate of childbearing by unwed mothers tripled from 1940 to 1958, a faster rate of increase than any time since. Contraception, once a radical political issue, became routinely incorporated into most marriages, furthering the acceptance of sensualism as a central part of personal identity during the decade.[11]

Postwar advertising gurus had long preached that one of the tasks of the free market in this era was "to demonstrate that the hedonistic approach to life is a moral, not an immoral, one." Although cultural arbiters tried to "contain" hedonistic sexuality within the framework of courtship and marriage, the tendency to push the envelope, as the Barbie doll certainly did, was built into the new consumer culture. *The Bob Cummings Show* (1955–59) depicted the life of a swinging photographer who played hanky-panky with the beautiful models he photographed. *Playboy* magazine initiated publication in 1953 with an article warning men to avoid "gold diggers" who wanted to trap them into marriage. Its columns offered advice about how to get sex without forking over a wedding band. Meanwhile, the standard Doris Day movie plot showed the quintessential nice girl of the decade on the verge of joyfully "giving in," until some accident intervened to expose the male's deviousness and make him realize that he really wanted to marry her after all.[12]

Sexual display, even for "nice girls," was not a stretch for 1950s culture, nor a rebellion against its basic values. Neither was the targeting of young girls' sexual fantasies and yearnings. Marketing experts had already discovered that "[a]n advertiser who touches a responsive chord in youth can generally count on the parents to succumb finally to purchasing the product." The marketing history of Barbie certainly confirmed this dictum.[13]

But the makers of Barbie were hardly radical innovators subversively harnessing the youth culture against parents. The Mattel toy company tried to convince mothers as well as daughters of Barbie's charms. The fundamental compatibility of the Barbie persona with 1950s gender norms and sexual mores is revealed in how easily they did so. Observing one mother change her mind about buying such an overly "mature" doll after the daughter commented on how well-dressed Barbie was, advertising consultant Ernest Dichter developed a marketing strategy based on "the doll's function in awakening in the child a concern with proper appearance."[14]

The strategy was a smashing success. If a certain amount of sexiness was needed to motivate a girl to become a "poised little lady," most moms were happily ready to make this concession.

The priorities of many little girls, as many memoirs in this volume point out, were quite different. Girls often made the concession of acting like little ladies in exchange for access to the sexual fantasies and play that Barbie permitted. And many girls certainly utilized their Barbie dolls, not to mention their Kens, in ways that violated their mothers' notions of proper sexuality or appropriate feminine passivity. But Barbie offered no challenge to unequal gender roles and the sexual stereotyping of women. She merely added to the arsenal of weapons that women could use to gain maneuvering room within the limits of such stereotypes.

As one episode of *Father Knows Best* in the 1950s advised a young woman: "The worst thing you can do is to try to beat a man at his own game"; it's far better to "just beat the women at theirs."[15] Barbie offered new ways of beating other women at the game of sexual commerce—and sometimes outsmarting men in the process. This was a game in which women manipulated men's preoccupation with female sexual appeal for their own individual advantage. It was a game where women tested their wits, explored their sexual power, and even acted out contempt or hostility toward men. But it was not a game that confronted men's social and economic dominance or offered women an identity independent of their sexual attractiveness. Rather than surmounting the contradictions of her era, Barbie quite literally embodied them.

DANGEROUS CURVES

1

*B*arbie's breasts have been a subject of interest and controversy from the very start; when Japanese doll makers continually made prototype dolls with nipples, the men at Mattel patiently filed them off before returning the dolls to Japan.

   Pamela Brandt's original essay "Barbie Buys a Bra" is a meditation on the ambivalent meanings those breasts had for her as a young girl. For M. G. Lord, Barbie's breasts represented terror and contagion, concepts she explores in this excerpt from her book, Forever Barbie: The Unauthorized Life of a Real Doll. *In "Teen Idol: Growing Up with Growing-Up Skipper," Leslie Paris examines a short-lived but fascinating Barbie offshoot: a Skipper doll who, with the crank of an arm, actually grew breasts.*

BARBIE BUYS A BRA

Pamela Brandt

*B*arbie had breasts. This was one undeniable and intriguing fact about her. My friends and I were not interested in Barbie's clothes. As soon as we shut the door, we stripped our Barbies of all finery, throwing the gauzy ballgowns and the polka-dotted pinafores into a small pile in the center of the floor. Then we posed our naked Barbies in a variety of ways, arms twisted coyly behind their heads, legs crossed demurely at the knees, busts jutting out, innocent facsimiles of *Playboy* centerfolds. We weren't interested in any other part of the anatomy but Barbie's breasts. They were perfect. None of us had ever seen perfect breasts. What we saw on our mothers and grandmothers ranged from flat to sagging half-filled air bags. When we stroked Barbie's breasts with our fingers, there was no erotic thrill but the satisfaction at finding something well made. For burgeoning adolescents who could find fault with every inch of our bodies, there was something reassuring about Barbie's perfection. We never thought her body was out of range. With hard work we could achieve that same uplift, the graceful swell, breasts that were like two mountains I once saw in Vermont, only flesh-colored instead of green.

Barbie didn't have nipples. Her breasts were uninterrupted by that bumpy reddish discoloration, rather like a reaction to poison ivy. I hated my nipples. They hurt when I bumped into things and when I was cold the ends would grow erect and boys would point at my shirt. My mother was beginning to insist I buy a bra. I was only in fifth grade at the time and not enthusiastic about the prospect. Barbies didn't wear bras. They didn't need to wear any artificial contraption of wires and hooks. My mother's own brassiere looked like an instrument of torture. The only other woman I knew who didn't wear a bra was my friend Cordelia's mother; she worked for Legal Aid and often went barefoot. Yet Cordelia's mother's breasts always hung low in her shirts and never stopped slowly swinging. It was hard to concentrate on anything else when you were talking to her. They seemed to swing in a slow rhythm, almost like the pendulum of a clock. I wondered if the judge had trouble listening to Cordelia's mother defend her clients in court. Barbie's breasts, unlike Cordelia's mother's bouncing bosoms, did not move. Their stability and solidity were impressive.

For me, the problem was nipples, not support. I knew nipples were there so babies could get milk from mothers, but since I didn't intend on having any babies I didn't see the point. White and yellow substances flowed out of these nipples and they didn't smell or look very nice. Nipples were ugly, and that was why Barbies didn't have them. Also, she had no children and didn't need them. Already, at the age of eleven, we were learning from Barbie that inescapable and essential parts of our body were unnecessary and unattractive.

My mother suggested that I buy a bra. I refused. A bra meant that I had to grow up and be a teenager. Teenagers couldn't play with Barbies and hide from the real facts of life. I wasn't yet ready for boys, though I judged from the catcalls in gym when I had to jump up and down that the boys were ready for me. Then there was a letter from the headmaster, explaining that certain modes of dress had to be observed. There would be no distracting lack of attire. Every morning the homeroom teacher would run her fingers down the back of girls in order to ensure that certain precautions had been taken. I wondered what Cordelia's mother would say about this new regulation. Cordelia herself didn't have to worry; her chest resembled our Ken dolls more than our Barbies.

The war was on. Every night I would cover my nipples with masking tape, hoping by morning they would be flat. Yet my nipples, and breasts, didn't go away, and one hot afternoon in June my mother marched me into the cool and fragrant first floor of B. Altman's. The women selling the perfume and cosmetics all looked like my Barbies, tall and thin and blond, not a nipple in sight behind their smooth silk shirts. "That's because they're wearing brassieres," my mother informed me, running her palms over her own well-supported bust.

The salesladies in the lingerie department on the sixth floor did not resemble Barbies. They were all middle aged or older with great sagging breasts that seemed to be engaged in a struggle with their undergarments. I'm sure their brassieres did their best to control all that sagging flesh, but somehow it was too much for even the experts at Playtex. They all wore shapeless flowered dresses that reminded me of my grandmother's housecoat. I was shocked at the sudden dip of sophistication; I could have been stranded near the bathhouse at Brighton Beach.

"She needs a bra," my mother said, interrupting a cluster of saleswomen complaining about the lack of air-conditioning on the upper floors. I had originally assumed my nervousness made me warm; now I realized that the ceiling fans did nothing more than just move thick warm masses of air against each other. Unlike the first floor, the scent here was sour—clammy armpits and hairspray.

"I can see," one saleswoman said, staring openly at my chest. I moved away, feeling my face flush. She walked toward the dressing room and slid open a red curtain. "Why don't you come in here, dear," she crooned, "and take off your shirt."

Barbie would never submit to such humiliating treatment. My mother marched on, as if it were perfectly normal for strangers to command her daughter to strip. The saleswoman had dyed orange hair and bright orange lipstick that almost matched. She told us her name was Marsha.

The dressing room floor was littered with crumpled bits of tissue paper and shiny pins that looked menacing to me, like tiny daggers. My mother told me to keep my sandals on and looked twice before she sat down. She waited for me to take off my shirt and then my trusted ally—my white undershirt. I slowly unrolled it belly up and then swiftly pulled it over my head. I cupped my hands over my breasts and felt tears prick at my eyes. I hated my breasts. Unlike Barbie's, the left one was larger than the right. Not only was I asymmetrical, but my nipples were different colors, the left one dark rose while the right one was a lighter shade, almost cotton-candy pink.

Marsha drew the curtains back so sharply that I thought they would rip. "Let me see," she said, a pin stuck in the corner of her mouth. Without warning, she reached over and grabbed my right breast as if it were a grapefruit, weighing it in the powdery creases of her hand. "Big for her age," she remarked, taking the pin out of her mouth.

"That's why we're here," my mother answered, her voice bristling. She had already looked at her watch twice and was clearly regretting her decision to come to B. Altman's. A store like Bloomingdale's would have had younger, trendier, and quicker salesgirls.

"I'll be right back," Marsha said, clumping away on her brown thick-soled shoes. She wore blue mascara that reminded me of my Barbie doll. Barbie's lashes, my friends and I had discovered, were the same shade as her eyes. I moved away from my mother, still cupping my breasts. The imprint of Marsha's fingers still felt fresh.

Marsha returned with a pile of what looked like twisted hangers wrapped with white bandages. My eyes filled with tears again; I wanted lace and flowers. My mother finally noticed my discomfort and quickly started talking about the importance of support. I imagined if Barbie wore a bra, it would look like a beautiful white rose blossoming across her chest.

Marsha made me bend down; my breasts hanging like two deflated balloons. She inserted each breast swiftly and snugly in a cup, as if she was scooping up two mounds of ice cream. When I stood up, way too fast, the blood rushed to my face and I felt suddenly dizzy. The brassiere scratched me the same way my black wool tights did. "There, it fits," Marsha remarked, her clawlike fingers pushing and pulling me into the contraption. My mother's eyes turned misty. "This is how I'll feel at your wedding," she told me, grabbing a clump of white tissue paper to blow her nose.

All I could see in the mirror before me was what looked like two blindingly white Styrofoam cups.

The heat of the small dressing room began to push at my chest. The loudspeakers blared with an announcement concerning a lost child; next door two teenage girls giggled. Suddenly I unhooked the bra, threw it on the floor, and grabbed my undershirt. "Leave me alone! Get out!" I shouted, hiding my face behind a veil of white tissue paper. My breasts hurt. More than anything else at that moment, I wanted my Barbie. I wanted to show my mother, to show Marsha, that this was the way girls were supposed to be, that breasts were not things to be clamped down and shoved up but left alone, soaring and free. My undershirt got caught around my neck as I hastily shrugged it on. The cotton felt soft and cool and still smelled of bleach. My mother touched me briefly on the shoulder, but I pulled away. Later, in the taxi, she surprised me with a pack of Lifesavers from the bottom of her bag. I ate only the cherry-flavored ones, the sweet syrup making my whole mouth ache.

*I*n spite of many rolls of masking tape, my breasts kept growing and I have graduated from minimum support to minimizer bras guaranteed to take an inch and an half off your bustline. Barbie's breasts, I notice in the stores, are still the same size and are still nipple-less. My own Barbies were thrown out long ago. Somehow I could not allow my first bra and my Barbie collection to coexist. They canceled each other out. Whenever I looked at my Barbies, I felt ashamed. Her breasts would never have nipples. Her breasts would never need support. Barbie was incapable of growing up. I was changing, growing, and for the first time felt angry. She wasn't so much a girl or a woman but an entirely different sex altogether. Barbie would never belong. Sometime that week I wrapped my Barbies up in my no-longer-needed collection of undershirts and dropped them in the bin for the back elevator man to pick up. Maybe he would discover them and present them to his own daughter. Or maybe Barbie would end up in the trash compactor, her body crumpled into a small, flesh-colored ball.

I have long since learned that Barbie will not go away. She will always be with us. She is as much a rite of passage as kissing your first boyfriend, figuring out how a Tampax works, and, of course, buying your first bra.

ELEGY FOR MY MOTHER

M. G. Lord

At thirty-seven, I am a five-foot-six, 123-pound, tolerably fit woman whose knees and elbows are considerably more prominent than her breasts. At the same age, my mother was, by most people's definitions, a beauty: five feet ten, 132 pounds, and possessed of breasts that in their size and shape resembled Barbie's. They didn't droop or sag; nor did their size—38-C—interfere with her ability to win at sports. Even in her forties she could swim faster and hit a softball harder than people half her age. No doubt you assume that I will write about how her perfection placed me in competition with her and, by extension, all women; how I ached to have 38-C breasts; and how every month when *Vogue* arrived I pored over pictures of Verushka begging, "Dear God, please make me look like her." Nothing, however, could be further from the truth.

When I was eight years old and my mother was forty-six, she had a mastectomy. Her experience with cancer did not have the happy ending that Ruth Handler's did. It was a prelude to chemotherapy, more operations, and, six years later, death. This was before the age of reconstructive surgery, political activism, and the life-affirming defiance that one sees among breast-cancer patients today. The illness was shrouded in secrecy, almost shame.

As her health deteriorated, her remaining breast mocked her. It hovered there—flawless—next to her indignant red scar. What it said to me was: You do not want Barbie's breasts; the last thing on earth you want are Barbie's breasts. I associated them with nausea, hair loss, pain, and decay. I associated them with annihilation. I believed myself blessed when nature didn't provide them.

True, at sixteen, when I had my first serious beau, I felt vaguely shabby that his gropings were so meanly rewarded; but the shabby feeling quickly passed. I was alive and hoped to remain so. In my mind, small breasts would make this possible; they seemed somehow less vulnerable. Of course, not every little girl's mother has a mastectomy, but many do. Since 1980, 450,000 women have died of breast cancer. In the decade of the nineties, an estimated 1.5 million women will be diagnosed with the disease, and one-third of them will die.

These grim statistics suggest that daughters of breast-cancer patients are far from an insignificant minority. But I suspect, as a consequence of the disease's historical invisibility, the experiences of breast-cancer daughters have often been ignored by so-called body image experts. When I heard *Beauty Myth* author Naomi Wolf say on National Public Radio, "We were all raised on a very explicit idea of what a sexually successful woman was supposed to look like," I wanted to shout that another "we"— millions of breast-cancer daughters—had had a very different experience. When Wolf said "the official breast" was "Barbie's breast," I muttered aloud, "Speak for yourself, lady." Not all women respond in a crazed, competitive, Pavlovian fashion to pictures of models or the body of a doll. And it's demeaning to suggest that they do.

My Barbie play was as idiosyncratic as my childhood. I remembered nothing about it until four years ago when my father got my dolls out of storage and shipped them to me. Tucked away since 1968, the vinyl cases seemed innocuous, yet I kept finding reasons not to open them.

I wonder if archaeologists hesitate, mid-dig, before making their discoveries, if they falter outside tombs the way I fumbled with the clasp of Ken's mildewed sarcophagus. When, after several tugs, the latch finally gave, I dropped the case, bouncing Ken onto the floor. I reached for him, then froze. He was wearing Barbie's low-cut, sequined "Solo in the Spotlight."

Nonchalant, he gazed at me, radiating what Susan Sontag has called the "androgynous vacancy" behind Greta Garbo's "perfect beauty." If Mattel had intended to model him on the Swedish actress, it couldn't have done a better job.

My Midge, by contrast, was laid out spartanly in her original carton: a mere sidekick, she didn't have a fancy case. At least she looked comfortable, wearing what I would have worn for twenty years in storage—Ken's khaki trousers, navy blazer, and dress shirt.

Then there was Barbie—blond ponytail Barbie—wearing tennis whites and a sweatshirt in her glossy red valise. Her cruel mouth, still haughty, brought back memories. I remembered a fight after which my mother grudgingly bought me fat-cheeked, blotchy Midge. I remembered a second fight after which she bought me perfect Barbie and Ken. And I remembered Midge's ordeal. Midge didn't seduce Ken—that would have been too obvious. She became his platonic pal, introducing him to a new pastime: looking more Barbie-like than Barbie.

I was tempted to slam the cases, to squelch the memories, but I rummaged farther. My dolls had not been cross-dressed in a vacuum. It had happened during the years of my mother's illness; years of uncertainty, of sleepovers at friends' houses when she was in the hospital; years which, until I opened the boxes, I had forgotten. But as I picked through the miniatures, why I did what I did became less of a mystery.

My Barbie paraphernalia was a museum of my mother's values. Arrayed together, the objects were a nonverbal vocabulary, the sort of language in which John Berger urged women to express themselves. Except for "Solo," which a friend had given me, the language was hers.

A chemist who fled graduate school long before completing a Ph.D., my mother was a casualty of the Feminine Mystique. She had stopped work to become a fifties housewife and hated every minute of it. She didn't tell me "Housework is thralldom," but she refused to buy Barbie cooking utensils. She didn't say "Marriage is jail," but she refused to buy Barbie a wedding dress. What she did say often, though, was "Education is power." And in case I missed the point, she bought graduation outfits for each of my dolls.

Nor did she complain about her mastectomy. I sensed the scar embarrassed her, but I never knew how much. Then I unearthed Barbie's bathing suit—a stretched-out maillot onto which my mother had sewn two clumsy straps to keep the top from falling down.

That sad piece of handiwork spoke to me in a way she never had. It spoke not of priggishness or prudery, but of the anguish she had felt poolside and why and she rarely ventured into the water. It spoke of how she felt herself watched—how all women feel themselves watched—turning male heads before the operation and fearing male scrutiny after it. It spoke of pain and stoicism and quiet forbearance. It broke her silence and my heart.

When things of aesthetic power—say, the Vietnam Veterans Memorial—have emotional resonance, the resonance feels right. But I cannot tell you how strange it was to ache with grief over a bunch of doll clothes. Or to find in a Barbie case a reliquary of my mother.

I forced myself to study Ken masquerading as Steichen's portrait of Garbo; Midge looking like a refugee from a boys' boarding school; even Barbie looking more Martina than Chrissy. (Barbie wore a tiny tennis skirt, but it was under *Ken's* sweatshirt.) I concluded that I'd been one messed-up kid.

But as I explored the mess, I came to realize that, given my environment, it would have been far flakier not to have cross-dressed the dolls. It wasn't just my mother's message that a woman's traditional role was loathsome; it was all the weirdness and fear floating around the idea of breasts. I don't think Midge's sartorial inspiration was Una Lady Troubridge or Radclyffe Hall. I think it was terror. Femaleness, in my eight-year-old cosmos, equaled disease; I disguised Midge in men's clothes to protect her. If her breasts were invisible, maybe the disease would pass over them. Maybe she'd survive. I even shielded Barbie, permitting her to show her legs but armoring her chest. Only Ken was allowed the luxury of feminine display; he had no breasts to make him vulnerable.

Teen Idol:
Growing Up with
Growing-Up Skipper

Leslie Paris

At first glance, Growing-Up Skipper seemed to be just another version of what Mattel, her maker, designated "Barbie's younger sister." Nine inches tall, with fluffy blond hair, this 1975 Skipper appeared on the fashion-doll scene dressed in a girl's ensemble: red headband, red leotard with removable blue collar, red-and-white houndstooth-checked miniskirt, red knee-high socks with matching flat Mary Janes. But Growing-Up Skipper was different from a run-of-the-mill Skipper; when her left arm was cranked backward, she grew three-quarters of an inch while smaller-than-Barbie breasts emerged from her formerly flat chest. Beneath that schoolgirl's demeanor lurked the body of a teen.

"Two dolls in one!" her product box announced. "Make Skipper doll grow: Turn her left arm all the way around, counter clockwise [sic]. See her grow slim and tall and curvy! For little girl Skipper: Turn her arm all the way around, clockwise. She's cute and young again!" This technological feat was made possible by the doll's sliding torso, composed of two layers: a softer plastic on top and a harder shell underneath. When her arm was turned, the action set her body into motion. The soft plastic rose up and away from the layer below, two cups set in the chest protruded out against the more flexible upper part, creating her breasts, and the underlayer of her torso became her new waistline. As the box promised, one could "Make her grow from a young girl to a teenager in seconds!" With a crank of the arm, cute became curvy. Skipper's postpubescent outfit, which arrived in her package, exemplified her new sophistication. She could replace the shorter skirt with an ankle-length "maxi" version. She traded in her collar for a fetching blue scarf, tied fashionably around her neck, and slipped her flat Skipper feet, sockless, into white platform sandals that accentuated her newfound height.

Of course, one could also play out the trajectory in reverse. Curvy could become cute again. In fact, Growing-Up Skipper's metamorphosis demanded such constant repetition, a back-and-forth motion between two bodies. In order to bring Skipper into her teens, she must always first be returned to girlhood. A mere crank of the arm away, each Growing-Up figure contained its bodily alternative. Each body had a meaning that depended upon its opposite configuration: the teenager that Skipper could become, the girl she had once been. And let us not forget the third doll, who existed only in the moment when Skipper's left arm was in motion. Whether expanding or contracting, this in-between doll *was* puberty, whose transitional body had not yet settled into either girlhood or teen life.

Although I didn't know it at the time, Growing-Up Skipper generated a certain amount of controversy upon her release. While the doll was successful enough to be produced through 1977 and to spawn a sequel, Growing-Up Ginger, she also elicited negative press. Her opponents characterized her as the pinnacle of tastelessness, akin to those baby dolls that soiled their diapers after being fed. This particular Skipper has since slipped to the edges of the official Barbie family history. Mattel's current press kit, which contains an incomplete "Barbie Genealogy," absents her from its list of product highlights. Nor has contemporary Barbie scholarship done anything to redeem the doll. M. G. Lord, in her witty and wide-ranging Barbie history, *Forever Barbie*, has suggested that Growing-Up Skipper "required from its owner a taste for the macabre." The doll, Lord claims, slipped into production at a moment when men managed the Barbie line, and it reflected a male rendition of a female coming-of-age: breasts, not blood.

Call me macabre, but as a girl I enjoyed this doll and its bloodless fantasy of adolescent development. Don't get me wrong; I can think of better role models for puberty, and none of them is in the extended Barbie family. I wouldn't claim that this Skipper was a useful preparatory tool for adolescence or that it nurtured my sense of the possibilities of womanhood. Indeed, as Mattel presented her, Growing-Up Skipper was quite bereft of higher goals, other than the conventional aspiration (still wildly popular today, although rarely attained) of becoming slim, tall, and curvy all at once. Hipless, bloodless, without a trace of hair below the head, this Skipper was hardly the embodiment of 1970s feminism, nor was she the doll version of *Our Bodies, Ourselves.* If she had sprouted pimples or underarm hair, she would have been a different doll. And Mattel remained rather coy about those breasts. The doll's packaging skirted the word altogether, relying instead on the euphemistic and discreet term *curvy.* Growing-Up Skipper's preoccupation with breasts and new clothes was not particularly unique in the Barbie universe. What was new was that she made so visible what Barbie only implied: that Barbie and her entourage serve, among other things, as tools to think through sexuality, and that they encourage girls (and boys, when they play with them) to stage their own fascination with bodily transformation and sexual identity.

I turned seven in 1975, so Growing-Up Skipper's debut corresponded with my prime Barbie years. I was the proud owner of this particular doll. I also owned a spin-off, the Growing-Up paper dolls. In the paper-doll version, a more dramatic partition between childhood and adolescence was enacted: two separate dolls, the girl and the teen. The paper dolls didn't even share clothes. Puberty and fashion had been severed irrevocably into a before and an after. Meanwhile, the plastic version, in her three-dimensional glory, highlighted the ambiguous in-betweenness of adolescence. One could choose to dress little Skipper in the platform sandals and scarf, or arrange the older Skipper in the demure collar. As for the "third" Skipper, busy moving forward and backward in corporeal time, she couldn't help wearing clothes marked a little too childish or mature for her changing body.

Of course, Skipper-style puberty was entirely predictable time after time, and was hardly representative of the complex biological shifts of puberty. But her body was pleasing in ways Barbie's could not match. For one thing, unlike her "grown-up" sister, Skipper provided evidence that breasts and normal feet could be combined in one doll body. Poor Barbie: Her strangely contorted feet were forever on demi-pointe, so that even when she went shoeless her feet cried out insistently for high heels. One of my earliest memories, circa 1972, concerns my own clumsy attempt to manage Barbie's footwear. Uncharacteristically, my mother had given me a Barbie outfit as a reward for something, now forgotten, that I had done. I recall sitting on the living-room carpet, trying to get my Barbie's new go-go boots onto her feet. This was no small task, as the boots—straight up to the knees à la Nancy Sinatra in "These Boots Are Made for Walkin'"—had little to do with the shape of Barbie's feet. My four-year-old hands could barely get the boots on, or subsequently extricate Barbie from her go-go bondage. Her delicate mules, on the other hand, slipped easily over her toes but fell right off again. Inevitably, they would be lost in the cracks of sofas and the shag of rugs, never to be seen again. Growing-Up Skipper, unlike her older sister, knew about comfortable footwear, and her shoes stayed put.

Purportedly, my generation of Barbie users had encountered an improved range of Barbie products with new powers of flexibility. In the late 1960s, Barbie had learned how to twist and turn at the waist. And as Lord points out, in a short-lived 1970 experiment she was even given flexible feet. Still, I found Barbie (who I imagined to be an adult, never an older teen) to be relatively rigid. She was plastic in the worst sense: hard, fake, a mass-market commodity. As such, there was little to love. I gave a deeper affection to stuffed animals and cloth dolls, huggable and soft creatures I could talk to, take to bed, or cry upon. Unlike these malleable toys, Barbie was easy to pose, and once in position, she stayed put. But with her blank stare and her frustratingly hard little body that remained impervious and unsullied by whatever was done to her, Barbie was hardly worthy of the same respect or gentleness due my one-eyed teddy bear. She was made for rougher stuff. I was constantly testing her limited range of motion, trying to make her go further, pushing her bodily limits by mashing her face or tilting it back as far as I could. Hoping to get Barbie to do cartwheels, I pulled at legs that only opened forward and backward, moving like limb-shaped scissors. I never defaced her with a marker, or cut off her hair, or bent her badly enough to tear off an arm. But I did things I knew would hurt a real girl, things I would never do to a more beloved toy. Later in my childhood I saved my stuffed animals, but I had no remorse about giving my Barbies away, and now I can't even remember exactly how many I once had (three? four?).

Who loved Barbies? Certainly not my mother, who made it clear that she didn't hold them in high regard. Dull, she insisted, and unimaginative. Given her general preference for more "educational" and "progressive" toys, it's not surprising that she has no memory of the Barbie boot occasion. In fact, I have upset her in my insistence that I owned a Barbie at the tender age of four. Someone else must have bought that doll for me; she says she didn't give in that early. The idea that at the very least she bought me those boots rings in her ears like an accusation: She must have been a bad mother. Actually, I remember being especially grateful on those occasions that my most mainstream desires were fulfilled. In any event, I do remember buying some of my

Barbies myself, with my grandmother's annual birthday gift of ten dollars in hand. I don't remember who picked out Growing-Up Skipper, and my mother, unsurprisingly, has no memory of this particular doll. As for my father, he lived in a world entirely outside of Barbie purchases and activities (except for the time that, as a joke, my mother presented *him* with the Mod Ken that she meant for my sister and me; his grimace, as though he had been handed a dead rat, said it all). For my parents, Barbie was a phase to be tolerated, not a place to linger.

As for me, I yearned for Barbies, I sighed over toy catalogs, and I lobbied unsuccessfully for Barbie's Town House. But desire and affection are, of course, not always one and the same; once I got the dolls home, their hermetic little bodies were fair game for anything I could dream up. My best friend and I sometimes enacted elaborate Barbie sex and torture fantasies that were anything but dull, in which the Barbies were kidnapped by an evil man and taken to a distant cave (my friend's neatly made bed) for torture, spanking, and assorted debauchery. In play, we enacted a potent mixture of domination, pleasureful naughtiness, and our worst fears about strange men, kidnapping, and assault. Or else, more sedately, we sent the Barbies out exploring in the jungle of our backyards, or dispatched them to school, or made them dance elaborate routines designed to minimize their lack of flexibility. Much of the time, they lay unused; my life was full of competing play opportunities such as running around in parks, dressing up, making flower "potions," reading, and going swimming. Further, unlike other dolls that I named with care, my Barbies were only worthy of provisional names. They were all just "Barbie," an indication of how successfully Mattel had branded them, but also of their limitation as objects of individual affection.

The only one I remember with any clarity is Growing-Up Skipper. In this doll, the inherently displeasing limitations of Barbie's anatomy had been partially transcended. Skipper's plastic body could be reimagined as a kind of plasticity, an openness to various possibilities. Unlike the body of her full-grown (perhaps overgrown) sister, hers actually exhibited a significant reaction to being touched. There was also something devious in what she did. Somehow, this blond, blue-eyed white girl, who came dressed in patriotic red, white and blue (although at the time, growing up in Canada, her Bicentennial-era patriotism was somewhat lost on me) turned out to be a freak. Like an exhibit at a circus sideshow, she combined conventional good looks with a special, strange talent: See Girl Turn into Teen—and Back Again! In her bizarre performance of sexual development and regression, Skipper called attention to the sexuality of the whole Barbie clan. She disrupted the notion that Barbies "just came that way." She highlighted the artificiality and constructedness of her coming-of-age, and she insisted that puberty itself was a performance. With her left arm raised high, she articulated a "middle space" of bodily flux and instability. Growing-Up Skipper not only tattled on her family's obsession with breasts and bodies, she unknowingly enacted late-twentieth-century feminist theory.

Perhaps the imposition of breasts on a seeming girl-child appears unfortunate. But in my play crowd, *all* Skippers, breasts or no breasts, were inherently endowed with some degree of sexuality. I imagined them to be about twelve years old; from a second-grade perspective, that was fairly advanced in age, but close enough to imagine. Like the sixth-grade girls in my elementary school, Skipper was mature enough to be a hallway monitor, wear the latest styles, and have a boyfriend. She was old enough to participate in whatever Barbie was up to—be it Rock Star, Poolside Vacation, or Sex Queen. The Growing-Up fantasy did not "make" Skipper into a sex object, nor did it create sexuality where none had existed in the Barbie clan. But it did expose the sexuality of our dolls and of our own lives as girls. By the age of seven, my friends and I saw, with both fear and excitement, how quickly we would be expected to grow out of girlhood into a sexualized adolescence.

In this sense, Growing-Up Skipper was a prescient doll-child. Moreover, she cloaked in play just how intensely the desire for bodily transformation can figure in the lives of actual girls and women. The doll's two modes are reminiscent of female struggles to change and perfect their bodies: plastic surgery (which "magically" allows for breast augmentation and stomach reduction) and anorexia (which enacts the return to a prepubescent body). One could read this Skipper's breasts-and-height puberty as an object lesson in female display and retreat, and Skipper herself as a fetish object for the doctrine of female self-improvement and bodily self-criticism. She blithely acted out a widespread fantasy: the ability to make one's sexual markers more or less visible at will, to grow or shrink in height, and to pass through physical transformation painlessly, with a smile.

Yet the doll was never simply a tool for teaching girls how, following Skipper's example, we could both become Barbies and revert to little-girl cuteness. I liked this Skipper because she was sexy without being overwhelming, and unlike her older sister, she responded positively to being touched. She encouraged me and my friends to put one hand on her chest to feel the breasts shoot out, while the other hand cranked her arm. Just below the surface of the doll lay her sneaky, risqué thrill: a speculative interest in female sexual development, which literally stirred up the doll's chest while stirring up little girls.

In the fall of 1996, when she taught "Ideal Bodies: The Modern Nude and Its Dilemmas," her advanced art seminar at Williams College, art historian Carol Ockman had her students read Kenneth Clark's classic book The Nude: A Study in Ideal Form *as well as all the available literature on Barbie. She wanted them to consider the ways in which Barbie's body is both ideal—that is, existing outside of time—and yet real, too. Her essay "Barbie Meets Bouguereau" grew out of the seminar—and owes a debt to the work of her students. The version that appears here was adapted from Ockman's original slide lecture. She takes a very literal look at the naked bodies of Barbie and Ken, and compares them to nudes, both painted and sculpted, of the past. In so doing, she probes at deeper meanings contained in traditional depictions of the human body and explains how Barbie's body is paradoxically timeless and yet utterly of its moment.*

Barbie Meets Bouguereau: Constructing an Ideal Body for the Late Twentieth Century

Carol Ockman

Love it or hate it, Barbie has been embodying ideal femininity for forty years (figs. 1, 2). Her role as "the most potent icon of American popular culture in the late twentieth century"[1] coexists with vituperative criticisms of the very body underpinning that success. For recent, and rather skeptical, authors, Barbie is at once an ideological sign for commodity fetishism, rigid gender definitions, and a hegemonic vision of heterosexuality.[2] This essay scarcely contests such assessments, but its focus, at least in part, is more strictly art historical. What I would like to explore is Barbie's complicated status as ideal body. It's obvious that Barbie's is not a realistic body but a fantasmatic one. For example, when the doll's measurements are compared to those of the average military woman, as they were in a study done in 1988, Barbie's body was six inches taller and slimmer at all points than the average WAC. Although Ken's body was also thinner than that of the average male soldier, Barbie and her female friends and relatives were all farther from the female norm than were Ken and his male cohorts.[3]

$\mathcal{B}$arbie's body has long been criticized because it is too tall and too thin, because it has outsize breasts and nonexistent hips, and because the feet are molded in the constant expectation of high-heeled footwear. More serious for critics than the disparity between such a body and the female body as they know it, however, are the possible effects of such an ideal on the young girls who measure their own developing bodies against the doll's. Barbie's body, and the fashion mania that accompanies it, might be said to crystallize the dilemmas of femininity and of the female body in late-twentieth-century North America and, increasingly, in Europe and elsewhere. Yet there is a paradoxical relationship between the knowledge that Barbie's body is unreal and the curious way it has been naturalized as ideal. In fact, this body, with its broad shoulders and wasplike waist, more transvestite than woman,[4] has the effect of making those bodies that don't resemble it seem abnormal.

Without question, Barbie has one quality that merits the term *ideal,* and that is timelessness. If her longevity and popularity are any indication, Barbie's body is perfect. Unlike Ken's body, which has had two radically different incarnations since he was originally introduced in 1961, Barbie's body has not changed dramatically since she first appeared at the New York Toy Fair of 1959 (fig. 1). Barbie's and Ken's relationship to the ideal becomes more anomalous when we think about the relationship between the nude and the ideal proposed by Kenneth Clark in his classic text *The Nude: A Study in Ideal Form,* published three years before Barbie's creation and in its eighth edition by 1990. Clark's definition of the nude is well known. Invented by the Greeks in the fifth century, the nude evokes balance, well-being, modesty, and decorum. It is not a living organism but the body re-formed, distinguished as much for its physical perfection as for its spiritual qualities. According to Clark, the realist nude, such as those depicted in nineteenth-century French paintings like Manet's *Olympia*, and the stylized nude we find in medieval images, fail as nudes. Clark's predilection for Greek art also has the effect of discounting Japanese and photographic nudes. Even if Clark would assuredly have banished Barbie and Ken from canonical nudity, his reasons for doing so have something more to tell us about the curious space they occupy between the ideal and the real.

Barbie and Ken dolls are made so that those who play with them, and here we are talking overwhelmingly about young girls from the ages of three to ten, take off the dolls' clothes so they can put them on again (figs. 3, 2). When we remove what Barbie and Ken are wearing, the first thing we notice, in light of Clark's definition of the nude, is the complete lack of balance and well-being in these bodies. Interpret as you will the fact that, since 1972, Aldo Favilli, the former restorer of sculpture at the Uffizi, has been the director of the sculpture department at Mattel. In these dolls, there is no overarching design, no sense that the parts are secondary to the whole. We are frightfully aware of the joints, for example, and let's not even mention the briefs to which Ken is condemned in perpetuity or Barbie's lack of nipples. The conclusion to be drawn from observing these bodies in the buff is simple. Barbie and Ken are not nude; they are simply without clothes. The nude, of course, doesn't need clothes; she (or he) is perfect in her nudity. Let's take two examples of the ideal, albeit imperfect ones in Clark's formulation, when compared to Greek art (figs. 4, 5). The bodies of Michelangelo's *David* and Bouguereau's Venus seem completely natural in the nude. Barbie and Ken, on the other hand, look much better dressed.

The fact that they are not nude, but without clothes, scarcely hampers their ability to function as ideal bodies, Barbie's in particular. With the exception of temporary modifications, such as permutations of the doll that enable more movement than the frozen arms and legs normally permit, her body has remained virtually a constant. It is precisely this capacity to represent the ideal but not the nude that is interesting. For at its heart lies a tension between the ideal and the real, visible, for example, in the naked body's joints, which make one conscious both of materials and structural function. As evidence of Mattel's enormous success in constructing Barbie as an ideal body, I offer two origin stories to highlight the centrality of fantasy both in the doll's conception and in the games people play with her.

First a cautionary note: Barbie was invented by a woman, Ruth Handler. Handler, a director of Mattel, together with her husband, Elliot (the "el" in Mattel, together with "Matt" from his partner, Harold Matson), had watched her daughter, Barbara (she also has a son named Ken), play with adult paper dolls and wanted to make an adult doll in three dimensions (fig. 6). On a trip to Germany, Handler supposedly saw a doll called *Bild Lilli*, sold principally in smoke shops as a kind of three-dimensional pinup. Based on a comic-strip character that appeared in the German newspaper *Bild Zeitung*, *Bild* Lilli had a ponytail, feet molded into high heels, and clothes for all occasions. The principal narrative of the comic shows Lilli, scantily clad, in situations where she is taking money from a man. Unlike Barbie, *Bild* Lilli was not made for children but for men, who displayed her on the dashboard of their cars and, more bizarre still, gave her to their girlfriends instead of flowers or chocolates. Handler decided to reinvent this pornographic caricature as the all-American girl. Enter designer Jack Ryan, great American playboy, husband of Zsa Zsa Gabor and others, and inventor of the bodies of the Hawk and Sparrow missiles during the Cold War. In the context of this period, so full of the terror of nuclear annihilation, Barbie became a symbol of prosperity. As an exemplary American product, much like the house in the suburbs, Barbie simultaneously represented and guaranteed American freedom and democracy. But what role, one might ask, do Barbie's torpedo breasts and the Lilli prototype play in this discourse of nationalist heroism, a discourse of the ideal?

One might say that the genius of Mattel consists in having invented a feminine body capable of fascinating the popular imagination (and here I refer to the power to stimulate both love and hate) for forty years. This long-lived fixation is fundamentally dependent on the "adult" character of Barbie. She was in fact marketed as the first "teenage" doll in the very years in which the term *teenager* came into existence. The fantasmatic erotic embodied in the supermissile breasts may well be central to Barbie's success as an ideal; even Kenneth Clark had to admit that the nude, in order to succeed, had to have an erotic component. At the same time, such a blatant sign of sexuality almost scuttled the doll when it was first introduced. Had it been up to the buyers at the toy fair, the ex-pinup/supermissile might never have been catapulted to stardom. Sears, Mattel's biggest client, categorically refused to buy Barbie, objecting to her too-overt sensuality. It was the consumers who launched Barbie's impressive career, the people who saw her on the shelves of toy stores. Unlike her prototype, Barbie gives the appearance of sexuality without sex itself. It is the fear of this reality—the reality that adults have sex—that frightened the buyers. But when designing an adult doll, in which sexuality is by definition part of the body fabric, it is simply impossible to avoid the issue of sex.

Barbie and those who populate her world might be understood as show-and-tell pedagogues whose job is to give daily lessons to young consumers about sexual development and sexual difference. Take the original Skipper, Barbie's little sister, introduced in 1964. Devoid of breasts, her pelvis nothing more than a squared-off block, it is quite obvious that she is a pre-adolescent. It's fascinating to note that more-recent versions of the Skipper doll have breasts like her older sister, perhaps a response to the increasing sexualization of adolescence, although the pelvic area remains undifferentiated. Inasmuch as the bodies of Barbie and Ken have to describe pubescence, the challenge of representing anatomy becomes that of representing sexual difference itself. Small wonder then that the sexual definition of teenage Barbie and Ken is my second story of origins.

Let's begin with one of Barbie's most remarked-upon attributes, her abundant breasts, and the fact, also much discussed, that they have no nipples. In the first stages of production, Japanese factory workers repeatedly added nipples to Barbie prototypes until designer Jack Ryan sent a model back with the nipples smoothed away (he used a nail file). If at first glance it appears that Barbie has the same preadolescent genitals of her little sister, a more careful look reveals this not to be the case (both in front and in back, there is definition we don't find in Skipper's body). Children playing with Barbie and Skipper can understand the distinction between an adolescent and a preadolescent body in explicitly sexual terms.

With the possible exception of the expurgated nipples, Barbie's sexed body did not present quite the challenge that Ken's did. In a sense, it would have been equally unthinkable not to represent Ken's genitals as to represent them. Or at least that seems to have been the opinion of Mattel's male executives who protested the bump proposed by Handler and Barbie's original wardrobe designer, Charlotte Johnson. The bump that appeared on Ken had a short shelf life; according to Erica Rand, it was eliminated because it cost less than the briefs he has worn ever since.[5] (Perhaps the method for excising the nipples was used.) The briefs were actually an ingenious solution, for they manage to give the impression that there's something to hide without ever showing what that is.

The overweening preoccupation of Mattel's male executives with Ken's bump may say as much, and probably more, about their discomfort with male genitals going public than it does about their concern with the likely psychic trauma such a bump might induce in "innocent" young girls, but it also raises the critical question posed by the teenage doll: "How does one teach sexual difference?" Here we come very close to Kenneth Clark's cautionary note about the nude: the need to contain the very eroticism it must have in order to function successfully. Barbie may be an expurgated version of Lilli, but she is also capable of having it both ways—that is, she can appear to be sexual while giving the impression of not being so for those who don't want her to be. The extraordinary legerdemain of Mattel consists of having transformed Barbie's highly sexualized origins from a liability to a major selling point. Lilli became Barbie, who became the ideal. This curious ideal might best be described as a kind of corporeal schizophrenia visible in the doll's huge breasts, which signify female sexuality, and the super-attenuated flanks, which tend to deny it. Barbie's physical form may derive as much from its prototype as from the exigencies of wardrobe. Consider for a moment the wasplike waist, so often reviled in the context of the doll's exaggerated thinness. Imagine, if you will, what happens when the four layers of fabric needed to make the inner seam of a waistband are added to a body that is one-sixth human scale. In other words, if it were less diminutive, Barbie's waist would be dramatically thicker than her hips. Ken's controversial bump experienced a similar type of downsizing. During its short life, it was much diminished in scale from the original conception in order to accommodate the zippers on his pants.

The image of a group of Mattel execs sitting around a big conference table discussing Ken's bump makes it clear, if we had any doubt, just how assiduously the company strategizes the intended effects of their products. It is equally clear, however, that Mattel has not wanted to prescribe in too explicit a way the functions of the doll or the messages it might convey. Take, for example, Handler's declaration about the aims of the doll when it was first released: "I designed Barbie with a blank face, so that the child could project her own dreams of the future onto Barbie. I never wanted to play up the glamorous life of Barbie. I wanted the owner to create a personality for the doll." And, another statement, which asserts: "Barbie was created so little girls could have choices about their futures."[6] These "choices," in my view, are provided by Barbie's innumerable accessories, and it is to these accessories and their function of particularizing the ideal body to which I would like to turn now.

When I speak of Barbie's accessories, I do so in a sense that is quite specific, and one I might add that is not to be confused with Erica Rand's use of the term in *Barbie's Queer Accessories*, published by Duke in 1995. By *accessories,* I refer to a broad spectrum of items, starting with clothes, those indisputable accessories that enable a series of identities as diverse as they are ephemeral, from leisure clothes to work clothes. I refer to Barbie's residences, beginning with the original Dream House of 1963 and followed by continually modified versions, to cars, starting in 1962 with the Pink Austin Healy, as well as environments as contemporary as they are varied. When I speak of accessories, I speak also of Ken, whose principal, if not exclusive, function is in relation to Barbie and not as an autonomous character in his own right. Following this same line of argument, all friends and relatives of Barbie that Mattel has produced—from Ken, introduced in 1961, to Christie, in 1963, to the Barbies of different races and nationalities introduced in 1980—are accessories.

Constantly invented and reinvented, these multiple accessories serve the function of particularizing Barbie's body and experience. One might even say that one of their predominant roles is to confer a historical identity upon a doll that is duly famous for her capacity to constantly change, as well as her paradoxically concomitant capacity to always remain the same. This distinction between accessories that particularize and the timeless body is analogous to the way clothing and decor function, for example, in portraits by the nineteenth-century artist Ingres. These works are renowned for an exactitude that enables scholars to date them based solely on fashion and furnishings. I want now to explore the inherent dualism in Barbie's modus operandi that depends equally on the immutability of her body and its up-to-the-minute accessories. In a way similar to Ingres's portraits, this discourse plays on the ideal and, more precisely, on the ideal as it relates to the real.

To better understand that relationship, let me offer a brief history of Barbie's accessories. The never-ending supply of clothes does more than attest to Barbie's initial career as a model. It stimulates a constant need for a doll whose changes are virtually all external to her form. The first twenty-one outfits Barbie wore owe a great debt to the couture fashion shows Charlotte Johnson, who designed them, was in the habit of attending. Popular culture takes the upper hand in the late 1960s, to be eclipsed by Hollywood in the 1970s. We see the arrival of Hollywood not only in the hunky physique that replaces Ken's slender nerd body of the early 1960s, but also in the new designs for the couple's heads. In fact, the faces of the new superstars have changed more than once. The pencil-thin brows, sloe eyes widened by makeup, and heavily rouged lips of Lilli's slightly X-rated physiognomy is replaced in 1965 by one that emphasizes the doll's large, innocent eyes. If in the sixties these look to the side, by the seventies they look directly out as we see them in the Superstar Barbie of 1977. Stereotypes of Southern California loom large in these new incarnations of Barbie and Ken, forever young, forever energized by daily visits to the gym or the beach. These variations, so tightly linked to up-to-the-minute fashion in different parts of the world, permit the so-called individualized projection envisioned by Handler, in which the child has the possibility "of creating a personality for Barbie" while they also nurture the child-consumer. Barbie and her pals have the power to move from one class to another at will: taking off in their camper one minute, only to relax in their town house the next, they have the infinite possibilities of social flux, with none of its attendant anxieties.

To our discussion of the tension between the ideal, a physical state outside of time, and the particular, a willed sign of the temporal, we must add one more fact: Together with the line of accessories that we've grouped under the rubric of friends and family, Mattel introduced a series of real personalities in the 1960s, including Twiggy, who was a model like Barbie, and the protagonist of the popular television series *Julia*, starring Diahann Carroll in the role of a nurse, mother, and widow. The reaction of Carroll, when she saw the doll for which she modeled, is revealing. Surprised that it didn't resemble her more, she commented tersely: "It looks like all the other Barbies."[7] The real dolls made by Mattel always demonstrate this type of compromise between the particular and the ideal. Inasmuch as the specificity (or realness) of Barbie and her accessories is illusory, it resembles what French cultural theorist Roland Barthes called the "reality effect." As he conceived it, the "reality effect" makes things look specific in order to shore up or naturalize the ideal.[8]

A banal but shocking fact about Barbie's accessories has uncanny relevance for any discussion of the "reality effect": All of Barbie's and Ken's friends (but not relatives, e.g., Skipper and Francie) have the exact same bodies so as to be able to wear their clothes [on the slight variations, see Ann duCille's "Barbie in Black and White," p. 127]. Even when the intent is that the Mattel dolls inspired by real people should be recognized by a large public—Michael Jackson, for example—Ken remains the prototype for men, Barbie for women. A particularly chilling case of life imitating art is that of Cindy Jackson (no relation to Michael), director of a company specializing in plastic surgery, who has had over twenty operations in order to "become Barbie."

Barbie's residences and environments, from the first dream house onward, also depend for their success on the "reality effect." The Dream House of 1963, the first of a series of nine, was introduced at the height of North America's romance with the suburbs. Open the portable carrying case and a living room with television, record player, closet, furniture, and a framed picture of that living doll, Ken, appear! The restrained modernism of the first houses is short-lived. "The Townhouse of 1974, with columns reminiscent of Tara and birdcage elevator"[9] exemplifies the eclecticism characteristic of the more recent residences. The rustic style develops (in tandem with a real interest in a return to the land) in the 1970s, thanks to the rustic cottage and the camper, complete with sliding door, baggage rack, camp chairs, and sleeping platform. In the same period, Mattel pays homage to the youth culture Woodstock put on the map in 1969 by introducing Café Now in 1971, decorated with posters preaching "Love," "Soul," and "Rock." Continuing to mine the latest in popular culture, Mattel issued "Barbie and the Rockers" in the eighties.

The production of environments at will parallels the frantic rhythm of consumer culture itself. Take, for example, Barbie Fashion Plaza, which houses the requisite bridal salon, plus generic clothing store, snack bar, beauty salon, and functioning escalator. Or the McDonald's, where Barbie and Ken work, with counter, menu, grill, and fry basket. Or the Bubbling Spa, equipped with towel, beach ball, and a pitcher with two glasses. Barbie's accessories—clothes, environments, fictive friends, and real-life companions—produce a kind of "reality effect" that naturalizes Barbie's body, rendering it paradoxically both authentic and timeless.

All this would amount to very little if it weren't for Barbie's enormous visibility and the success with which the doll and her accessories have colonized a large part of the world. In fact, Barbie has conquered so effectively certain parts of the world that it might be fair to say she structures them. Quite simply, the doll has become an integral part of our physical and metaphysical world: Physical in the sense that already in 1992 it was determined that if all the Barbies that had been sold were placed head to toe, they would describe the circumference of the earth four times. According to Mattel, Barbie has 100 percent name recognition among women with daughters between the ages of three and ten.[10] Barbie populates space in other senses as well, historically, through her careers as stewardess (1961) and astronaut (1965), and, more recently, through her increasing presence on the Internet. One can find a hallucinatory group of Barbie sites not sponsored by Mattel, among which I might mention all manner of fantastically reconstructed Barbie and Ken bodies, including "Liposuction Barbie" with the option of adding cellulite to Barbie's hips and thighs or the enhancement of the already ample breasts, as well as the elimination of these prostheses at will. There is also a growing selection of artworks inspired by Barbie, among them Barbie *Liberty*, inspired by Delacroix's *Liberty Leading the People* of 1830, and Barbie *Olympia* after the Manet painting of 1863, and in a more terrestrial manner, the multiple houses and environments we have already discussed. Given the reach of Barbie's spatial empire, it behooves us to ask again: "What are the lessons that Barbie's phantasmatic ideal body teaches?"

On the most basic level, it could be said that Barbie represents the values of white middle-class America. We've already mentioned that she conveys sexuality without sex. One could say that she also teaches heterosexual teenage rituals.[11] More obvious perhaps are the lessons she and her friends and family impart about grooming and fashion, a point often highlighted by Mattel. Barbie is meant to, or perhaps I should say *could*, teach all of these things, much as she could foster the importance of a tall, lean body, a body that, with few exceptions, has little physical mobility; in spite of the enormous variations that enable Barbie to have diverse careers, different color eyes and hair, even the varieties of skin tones and features that make Barbie multiracial, the ideal remains the white, blond, blue-eyed doll with the ideal body.

But there are less obvious lessons that Barbie teaches. As one consumer put it, "She owns a Ferrari and doesn't have a husband; she must be doing something right!"[12] In spite of a love story that has endured for forty years and a new bridal gown every year, Barbie has never married and she's never had children. It could be said that Barbie has something to teach us about independence. Jacqueline Urla and Alan Swedlund link the hardness of her body to ideas of mastery and control.[13] Given that Barbie depends so much on fantasy, it shouldn't surprise anyone that there are many visions of Barbie that have little or nothing to do with those authorized by Mattel, as purposely vague as those are. There are even Barbie actions, some of which have a certain fame in Barbie lore, including one carried out by the BLO, the Barbie Liberation Organization, whose acronym willfully parodies that of the PLO. A group made up of artists, professionals, and concerned parents, and led by a student at UC–San Diego, the BLO switched the voice boxes of Teen Talk

Barbie and G.I. Joe in 1993 so that when they were purchased and brought home, the first words uttered by G.I. Joe, and in falsetto, were "Let's go shopping!" Even if the BLO didn't exist, Mattel is incapable of controlling how Barbie is used. For all the little girls who suffer because they don't look like Barbie (which should be the overwhelming majority), there are those who deliberately construct their sense of self in opposition to the ideal personified by Barbie. This reaction against the dominant lessons Barbie teaches is one of the most promising directions being pursued by scholars who are theorizing gender roles that are not fixed but instead constructed and performative.

Nowhere is this reaction clearer than in the most disturbing images of Barbie my students and I have found on the Internet and elsewhere (fig. 7). These works place themselves in opposition to the interminably repeated messages about beauty, fashion, and consumption delivered by Barbie and her accessories. Often they demonstrate a rage that seems deliberately excessive. These works could be considered the artistic equivalent of the various mutilations inflicted upon Barbie by the young girls who play with her, including adding nipples, ripping off her head, or flushing the doll down the toilet. These actions resist the notion of Barbie as the all-American girl. Through their aggressive play, these girls, like the artists who made these sculptures, challenge the naturalized ideal that is Barbie's body either by insisting on the realities excluded by that body (for example, drawing the nipples back on) or by destroying it completely (ripping off its head).

In these sculptures, torture, even sacrilege, are made explicit. Despite visible signs of violence—nails that rupture the skin, blood that oozes from wounds—the doll continues to smile. Maggie Robbins recounts how difficult it was to hammer nails into Barbie's eyes as well as her shock, upon having done so, that the smile was still there. Instead of mutilating Barbie, Susan Evans Grove refers explicitly to violence against women in "Battered Barbie (But Ken's Sorry)."[14] By denaturalizing the ideal Barbie represents, these artists call attention to the power of real violence and to the power of imaginary violence. In doing so, they bring to mind the potent visual strategies of Cindy Sherman. In her untitled photographs from 1992, Sherman posed plastic hospital mannequins purchased via mail order from medical suppliers and made a kind of collage from body parts and occasional accessories (fig. 8). The emphasis on horror that we see increasingly in her work succeeds in annihilating any notion of an ideal body or nude. By rendering the ideal disgusting and suggesting the possibility of real violence, Sherman, much like these artists who re-view Barbie, may be said to criticize that real violence while utilizing its own power against it. The possibility of confronting the ideal with the real can be found in child's play (or, in the case of fig. 9, in adult's play) and in artistic production. If these works of fantasy can shock, they can also be cathartic. The fact of insisting on the real, of keeping it visible, prevents the naturalization of the ideal.

It is in this sense that the tension between the ideal and the real can be productive. If Barbie populates real space, then it is also true that she populates mental space. Many of the Barbie sites, guerrilla actions, and artworks inspired by Barbie offer resistance to the dominant vision of her spatial sweep. We can't know how long Barbie's success will last. While she reigns, the importance of inventing images that dispute her thrall and vie for the space she occupies cannot be underestimated; they have the possibility of changing both the real space and the mental space she has conquered or, at the very least, calling them into question. As long as that resistance is enacted or made visible, the tension between the ideal and the real will be as dynamic as it is visible.

History of American Girls, Joan Jacobs Brumberg details how the process of maturing has changed for girls in the course of the twentieth century. Unlike their counterparts in the Victorian age, "girls today make the body into an all-consuming project in ways young women of the past did not."[2] This obsession with the body, which includes attention to shape, skin, clothes, and hair, as well as a preoccupation with sexual desirability, has come about as a result of historical changes in our values and in the way we nurture our girls. First, our secularization as a culture has transformed the way we think about self-worth: We tend to focus on looks at least as much as on character, especially for girls. As Brumberg puts it, "[In the nineteenth century,] many parents tried to limit their daughters' interest in superficial things, such as hairdos, dresses, or the size of their waists, because character was considered more important than beauty by both parents and the community. And character was built on attention to self-control, service to others, and belief in God—not on attention to one's own, highly individualistic body project."[3]

Second, we no longer supervise and direct the activities of our adolescent girls with the same degree of attention. For better or worse, Americans in the nineteenth century were preoccupied with the sexual purity of teenage girls between the onset of menarche and marriage. The value of girlhood innocence "influenced Victorian mothers in their dealings with developing daughters, and it animated countless community efforts to monitor and supervise young women in single-sex groups designed to promote innocence and purity."[4] Such groups, which included the Girl Scouts, Campfire Girls, and Young Women's Christian (and Hebrew) Association, relied on "intergenerational mentoring";[5] grown women, often in their twenties, supervised teenage girls and felt that it was their responsibility to do so. Mothers today are less preoccupied with their daughters' sexual purity (teenage sex is widely accepted if not welcomed), and girls are given more freedom, freedom that can be a burden as well as a blessing, as they negotiate the dangers and seductions

Have you ever wondered why there are no old people in Barbie-land? No parents, grandparents, aunts, uncles, no one older than Barbie, whose age seems to shift between teenaged student and bright, young career gal. Wendy Singer Jones explores the implications of Barbie's agelessness—a state that allows her to be both self-sufficient yet abandoned—in "Barbie's Body Project."

BARBIE'S BODY PROJECT

Wendy Singer Jones

Although I'm writing for *The Barbie Chronicles,* I do not wish to enter the Barbie wars. These battles revolve around whether Barbie is a wholesome or destructive toy for girls: Does Barbie foster an unhealthy body image and a superficial ideal of womanhood? Does her essential racial Euro-whiteness (even in ethnic versions) marginalize little girls of color? Does she instill an ethic of consumerism? Or does Barbie enable imaginative play and provide a safe forum for girls to explore femininity and sexuality? I want to bracket the question of Barbie's effect on the little girls who play with her, and focus instead on what she has to tell their parents. The Barbie phenomenon, including dolls, books, and other products, has much to say about how our society conceptualizes growing up for little girls—what it means to enter American womanhood—as we approach the millennium, and as Barbie celebrates her fortieth birthday.[1]

The Barbie world accords with a disturbing paradigm of contemporary female adolescence. In *The Body Project: An Intimate* of a culture obsessed with sex and the body, and with the articulation of that obsession through advertising and peers. In short, the dismantling of an institutionalized and familial system of surveillance and nurturing has abandoned girls to a consumer culture that is all too ready to sell a multitude of body products—makeup, clothing, diet aids, depilatories, and so on—and to the peers who reinforce one another's mutual obsessions.

The Barbie product fits the body project. Although Barbie no longer pursues her career as fashion model exclusively—a career in which one's profession *is* a body project—her other identities are relatively crude palimpsests: You can take Barbie out of modeling but you can't take the model out of Barbie. A trip to my local Toys "Я" Us store in Big Flats, New York, revealed clearly that no matter what her putative career or focus, Barbie's main job is to work on her own body. Admittedly, the store did not stock the entire Barbie line, but as a midsized branch of the chain, it had a representative sampling: an aisle and a half devoted exclusively to Barbie dolls and products.[6] I divide these dolls into five categories. First, there are the special-edition Barbies including the Dolls of the World International Collection, the Star Trek Gift Set, Nostalgic Reproductions (of older Barbies), the Hollywood Legends Series (Barbie as various characters and actresses), and so forth. Since these dolls are sold primarily to adult collectors who are not interested in acquiring more outfits or other Barbie products, they are not especially germane to my analysis.[7] The next group consists of generic Barbies and friends, not identified with particular jobs or qualities, such as Sweetheart Barbie; Eatin' Fun Kelly, baby sister of Barbie (who comes in her high chair); Pearl Beach Barbie, dressed in a bathing suit; Becky, Barbie's friend in a wheelchair; and Totally Cool Ken, Surprise Gift for Barbie Doll (he holds a small decorative shopping bag in his hand, but as his title indicates, it is unclear whether this or Ken himself is the surprise gift). Next in specificity are what can be called theme or occasion dolls, still not identified with specific jobs but contextualized to a greater degree. Among these are two very popular

Barbie items, Birthday Barbie and Wedding Fantasy Barbie and Ken.[8] In the Gardening Fun—Barbie and Kelly set, the two sisters are dressed to till, while Holiday Sisters Barbie, Stacie, and Kelly are decked out for winter festivities. Horse Ridin' Barbie, attired in aristocratic riding gear, is ready for the chase; Movin' Groovin' Barbie is set to dance; and Charity Ball Barbie has elegantly girded herself for good works à la Princess Di. The next group of dolls, what I'll call the "body Barbies," are single-mindedly and unabashedly dedicated to particular body projects. Twirlin' Make-Up Barbie can color her lips, cheeks, and eyes. Bead Blast Barbie's work consists of beading her unbelievably thick, long hair; she comes with 101 beads, a tool for attaching them, and a brush. Cool Blue Barbie streaks her hair with "COOL COLOR STREAKS" ("Add a bracelet to my thumbring and hip nail color and I'm set for a party for my sister Teen Skipper")—ditto in pink for Perfect Pink Theresa, green for Extreme Green Teen Skipper, and purple for Purple Panic Christie. Workin' Out Barbie exercises to keep her perfect figure. Finally, there are the dolls with definite jobs or functions, including the official career Barbies. On my field trip, I met with Twirlin' Ballerina Barbie, Pilot Barbie, Olympic Skater Barbie, Dentist Barbie, Paleontologist Barbie, Teacher Barbie (whose dress, decorated with apples, pencils, and rulers, self-reflexively announces her profession, and wittily refers to another flamboyantly decked-out teacher, Ms. Frizzle of the *Magic School Bus* series), and University Barbie, dressed as a cheerleader and sporting different university logos (if you're lucky, you can buy the one for your college).

Despite Mattel's nod to feminism and women's achievements, the majority of Barbies and her female friends have activities and accoutrements that emphasize the body. While this preoccupation is most obvious in the "body Barbies," it is present, if more subtle, in many of the other dolls. That dress that is so important to Wedding Fantasy Barbie is in keeping with our cultural norms, since clothes constitute such a large part of the marriage ritual. But Barbie's birthday outfit is as dressy as her wedding gown. Although the official career Barbies are least likely to be identified with the body per se, many of their outfits are unrealistically sexy. Pilot Barbie's uniform is low cut and trimmed in bright pink, outlining her figure; Paleontologist Barbie wears hot pants rather than hiking shorts; Dentist Barbie wears a tightly belted, form-fitting white jacket over her minidress.

All the athletic Barbies—and I include traditional and nontraditional occupations for women (dancers, skaters, horseback riders, etc.)—are by definition focused on the body. It is true that women's athletic prowess can be empowering, but it nevertheless demands a narrow concentration of time and energy. And the difference between a necessary and an unhealthy emphasis on the body is often hard to detect: Witness the prevalence of eating disorders among dancers and gymnasts. Moreover, many of Barbie's sports depend on the spectacle of female beauty (who expects a football player to be lithe and gorgeous?).[9] Why is so much of Barbie's ability geared toward the physical? University Barbie is an especially interesting case: Barbie's college experience is defined by her cheerleading, another activity that relies heavily on women's bodies and looks. In an academic environment, where "mind" should at the very least have equal time with "body," Barbie still can't get away from her fashion-model mind-set.

The Barbie books follow suit. They present a fascinating means for "reading" Barbie. Licensed by Mattel, they portray the official Barbie—the girl Mattel wants the world to see— thereby providing a model of the correct way to fantasize about Barbie. They also allow Barbie to have some kind of interior life and to communicate values. Indeed, the Barbie of the books is the least superficial of the Barbies; her stories frequently have a moral, or attempt to teach ethics in some way. Yet even within the context of the "moral Barbie," these stories almost always emphasize Barbie's looks, and if she has a career, it is usually in one or another of the glamour industries. For instance, in *Very Busy Barbie*, Barbie is late to an interview for a job as a model for the Lily line of fashions because she rescues an elderly lady who has fallen out of her wheelchair.[10] This good deed prompts Ms. Lily to give the job to Barbie rather than Laureen, another model, because not only is Barbie beautiful, but she is also "a caring person." Laureen, who has long been jealous of Barbie for having won a swimsuit contest earlier, learns that "there was more to modeling than just beauty" (well, you could have fooled some of us!).[11] Against the grain of the entire Barbie project, the book asserts the superiority of character to looks. But Barbie still has the looks. And if she were ugly, she could save ten old ladies a day and it wouldn't make a difference to her career potential as a model.[12]

Many of Barbie's milieus evince a similar focus on the body beautiful. To be fair, body-neutral territories are available, such as the Lovin' Care Baby Center, a kitchen, a home office (presumably for Teacher Barbie), a movie theater, and various pink vehicles. Yet Barbie's environments often revolve around the spectacle of her spectacular body. All the bedrooms for the Folding Pretty House contain vanities, as if such an item were de rigeur for everyday dressing. The athletic Barbies possess suitable environments and accessories: Workin' Out Barbie can exercise at her very own Fitness Center. Western Stompin' Barbie (another rider) has her own horse. Barbie shops almost exclusively at clothing stores (bodily adornment) and supermarkets (bodily consumption)—is it coincidence that these are the venues most obsessed about by those who suffer from eating disorders? These include Shoppin' Fun with Barbie and Kelly, a grocery store; Fun Fixin' Supermarket; a Mini-Mart; a Kool-Aid Stand; Cool Shoppin' Barbie, a clothing store; and The Barbie Boutique ("It's the coolest boutique and café in town"). For the crowning touch, Barbie gets her hair done at the Shampoo 'n Style Salon.

The related Barbie products continue this emphasis and, even more important, extend the body project to the little girls who play with Barbie. I want to stress once again that I am not positing a simple cause-and-effect relationship between play and personality, but nevertheless, a tour of these products does suggest that such play is a precursor to, if not a cause of, the real body projects that will begin shortly before adolescence. This is not true of all Barbie paraphernalia, some of which simply bears the Barbie image, such as the slumber tent, the play house, bedding, knapsacks, lunchboxes, etc., but many more items revolve around bodily adornment. Even though I inventoried only one store, the list is quite long: Barbie Fancy Fingers (acrylic nails for children); Party Perfect Shoes (high heels); Barbie Stylin' Hair Wear; Barbie Purse Maker; My Very Own Wedding Fantasy Bride Dress Up; My Very Own Deluxe Beauty Gift Set; several jewelry-making kits: Beautiful Boutique, Treasure Box Trinkets, Alpha Beads; Barbie Jelly Shoe Designer; Super Talking Musical Make-Up Mirror; Talk 'n View Magic Mirror; Super Talking Purse Set, which comes with eye shadow and lipstick; a multitude of individual items of jewelry (watches, necklaces, rings, earrings); and My Very Own Vanity, which says it all!

Some of these toys blur the distinction between Barbie's world and the child's by including body products for each. Twirlin' Make-Up Barbie comes with acrylic nails for the little girl who plays with her. The "COOL COLOR STREAKS" for the Cool Blue Barbie dolls' hair is meant to be used by the child as well. Show Parade Barbie with Her Star Stompin' Horse comes with earrings. Among the most interesting of these items is a combination board book and toy entitled *Barbie's Special Night.* The book tells about Barbie's and Midge's preparation for the opening night of a concert hall. We see the dolls having their hair done, choosing dresses, bathing (well, wrapped in a towel after the bath), and finally, fully in situ at the concert hall:

It's curtain time. Barbie and Midge, dressed in their glittering gems, walk down the elegant staircase into the twinkling lobby. They can see their reflections in the mirrored walls, and they both look enchanting. They are ready to enjoy one very special night.[13]

Although Barbie and Midge are presumably about to attend a concert, culture is merely a footnote to the real work of self-display. The most important aspect of this evening is that the dolls "look enchanting." And "enchanting" is an overdetermined word here: It is uncanny that we see no one else in the concert hall, no one to interrupt this self-enclosed narcissistic moment of specular contemplation and exhibition. Barbie and Midge are eerily alone with their own perfect images. The book comes with an attached package of items: lipstick, necklace, and, most important, *a mirror.* How can we fail to read this as extending the narcissism of the body project to the little-girl reader?

*I*f Barbie epitomizes bodily self-fashioning, she is not entirely to blame. Where are the elders to guide her toward a less superficial view of herself and to protect her from the constant onslaught of consumer culture? In Brumberg's view, girls are at risk precisely because we have abandoned such mentoring: Girls today lack the close guidance of mothers, organizations, and older women that protected teenagers of an earlier generation. Barbie illustrates this lack, for Barbie lives in a world peculiarly devoid of adults, a world of peers and younger children. And although Barbie frequently advises her younger sister and their friends, especially in the Barbie books, such a world precludes the concept of guidance and intergenerational mentoring for Barbie herself. Perhaps Barbie, like her real-life counterparts, is so focused on her body because there is so little else to occupy her.

Such an argument does not depend on Barbie's literal age, which is obscure.[14] Barbie was certainly a teenager to begin with; the first catalog copy describes her as "a shapely teenage fashion model."[15] And in an early novel, *Barbie's New York Summer,* she bemoans being "sixteen going on seventeen."[16] But these days, she sometimes seems to be an adolescent, sometimes an adult. Barbie's Dorm Room and University Barbie suggest that she is in her late teens or, at most, her early twenties—in any case, she is still a student, and presumably dependent on adults until she graduates. The Toys "Я" Us Barbie wears a pink T-shirt that says, "I'm a Toys 'Я' Us Kid." But other scenarios suggest that she is already grown. This is true of all the career Barbies, although one can assume (as Mattel does about the Barbie's Wedding Fantasy), that such dolls represent Barbie's fantasies about future possibilities.[17] In any case, determining whether she's a teen or a grown-up depends on individual interpretation—she can be either. Barbie's houses (the Barbie Dream House and the Folding Pretty House) illustrate the liminality of Barbie's status. What's a teenager doing with her own house anyway?—she must be an adult. But these houses look like they were designed for teenagers, or even little girls, decorated as they are in that bright Barbie pink that no one past the age of sixteen could live with. And all the beds for the Folding Pretty House are single beds— Ken definitely does not stay over! If Barbie products for little girls dissolve the boundaries between Barbie's world and ours, the traffic in influence goes both ways. Girls might take up Barbie's body projects, but Barbie lives in a world of children's rooms.

By obscuring the boundary between adolescence and adulthood, Mattel makes it irrelevant. If Barbie is both a teen and an adult, but, at the same time, always Barbie, this makes teenagerhood as autonomous and self-sufficient as adulthood. Moreover, there is no transformation from one phase to the other. This is all too often the view of both teenagers and adults today, if for different reasons: Adults lack the time and means for effective mentoring, and anyway, teens themselves look primarily to peers. It is common knowledge that our children are growing up earlier and earlier, that we are, in effect, losing childhood. Barbie's shifting age epitomizes that loss.

Whatever Barbie's precise age, age itself is represented lopsidedly in the Barbie line of dolls, where no one is older than twenty-five at most. This is especially bizarre given the presence of Barbie's little sisters: Where are the adults who engendered these children? Where are Barbie's mom and dad? Although Mattel concedes that Barbie has parents, the company says as little as possible about them, and they have never produced the dolls.[18] The strange configuration of Barbie's family is particularly evident in the Barbie books. In *Girl's Best Friend,* Barbie lives alone with her three younger sisters, Skipper, Stacie, and Kelly, and there is no question the existence or absence of parents, despite the fact that Kelly is a toddler.[19] *Let's Have a Sleepover* inadvertently emphasizes this erasure of parents.[20] The story begins as Stacie's friend Emily gets ready to go to school and, later, to a sleepover at Stacie's house. One or both of Emily's parents appear in three of the illustrations, and they are obviously older than Barbie, probably in their early thirties. But when Emily gets to Stacie's house, guess who's in charge? Older people have strangely vanished from the scene, and Barbie takes over the parental function, helping Emily to overcome her homesickness. One can only suppose that Barbie is so remarkably capable that her duties never weigh heavily upon her, even though she lacks an older community to support, advise, and share the burden. But if the absence of such elders indicates Barbie's competence, it also signals the self-sufficiency of a culture of youth, in which the young can unproblematically lead themselves.

Yet such leadership is ultimately flawed. When it comes to mentoring her sister, Teen Skipper, Barbie is sadly lacking. She might teach the right stuff to younger children, but she teaches only body work to Skipper. The copy on the box for Extreme Green Teen Skipper shows how Skipper looks to Barbie for glamour wisdom: "I can't wait to brush on Extreme Green COOL COLOR STREAKS into my hair *just like my sister Barbie.* I'll cruise to the mall, show my teen friends my cool bracelet, thumbring and jammin' nail color and I'll be the buzz" (emphasis mine). If being a teen is all about working on your body so that you can show it off to your friends, then Skipper's training is obviously from Barbie. Such apprenticeship is the subject of one of the few books to feature Skipper, *In the Spotlight.*[21] Barbie, now a TV reporter on fashion news, is all set to interview Kelvin, a famous designer, when his model Nina is delayed at the airport. He asks Barbie to take her place, but she is the only reporter on the scene. Who will do the interview? Skipper comes to the rescue, acting as a cub reporter, while Barbie models the gown. But really, there's not much difference between them, since Barbie's true identity as a model was so thinly disguised from the start. Skipper successfully completes her first internship for a career in beauty that she will certainly pursue.

By way of contrast with the values of the Barbie world, we might consider another product of the same corporation: the Fisher-Price Dream Doll House, which comes with a mother, father, baby twins, and some basic furniture. Like Barbie, the Doll House invites consumers to enrich their play by purchasing a variety of supplemental products. But the emphasis of these products is very different. Doll House toys focus on creating a home rather than a self; they are about a family rather than an individual or series of individuals. Unlike Barbie products for the line of dolls, which consist mainly of clothes and accessories, most of the Doll House sets comprise additional furniture for designing the family's interior and exterior space. In a sense, the difference between the two product lines is the difference between mutuality and narcissism. Despite the presence of friends and sisters, the Barbie line stresses individuals rather than relationships, and it does so in a highly narcissistic mode, since "body work" is a prerequisite to any form of social interaction. In the Dream Doll House, the family is greater than the sum of its parts; with Barbie, it's always all parts. While it is clear that both product lines are in some sense about the joys of consumption, the Doll House abjures Barbie's narcissism and isolation. When your project is your house rather than your body, you're already thinking in communal rather than solipsistic terms.

Of course, Barbie, like the Doll family, does have a dream house, but it does not project this vision of interdependence and mutuality. The Barbie Dream House is all about Barbie, as the title suggests. With its signature pink decor, it is yet another accessory, designed to adorn the adorable. It is *Barbie's* house, not someone else's; it is Barbie's *dream* as well, although the child is included in this narrow vision, as the copy on the box indicates: "a special world for Barbie and you."

The difference in emphasis between the two product lines can be seen by comparing an occasion they both have in common: the birthday. The Doll House Birthday set comes with three little girls, a birthday cake, a table, two gift boxes, a birthday banner, a tape player, and (my personal favorite) a toy dollhouse. The only items of clothing are three removable shiny skirts, so that the birthday girls can dress for the occasion, but the set does not stress bodies or dresses. Birthday Barbie consists of the doll attired in an exquisite formal gown, whose extensive ruffles and flounces announce that dress occupies center stage on this occasion. Barbie's birthday is about looking good; the Doll House birthday is about having a party.

This difference in focus is evident in two additional aspects of the Doll House line, which surpass the limits of Barbie's world in important ways. First, the Doll House gestures toward the larger community in which it is situated. While it is true that Barbie ventures beyond the confines of her Dream House, she nevertheless appears to travel in a protective bubble of accessories and peers. The movie theater, for instance, is frequented by Barbie and friends alone. Who sells the tickets or runs the projector? But the Doll House family has their mail delivered by a mail carrier (a woman!), they go to the village vendor for ice cream on hot days, and a teenager comes to baby-sit the children. If each family member is part of a larger whole, the whole family is part of a larger neighborhood. Identities are contextualized and ultimately collective. Second—and this is crucial—the Doll House line includes figures *of all ages.* The ice cream vendor has gray hair. You can even buy grandparents. The Doll House world is intergenerational: Older dolls are there to guide the younger ones.

When I shared some of these observations with an executive at Mattel/Fisher-Price in an informal conversation, this person defended Barbie by pointing out that the Fisher-Price Dream Doll House is designed for a much younger crowd. Well, yes, but that is precisely the point. Why, when we think about play that revolves around teens (or even twentysomethings), do we necessarily think of clothes, accessories, designer bodies, and the requisite peers to appreciate them all? Because this is how our culture defines adolescence for girls. This is made clear through an instance of "crossover" in the two product lines, where Doll House and Barbie switch their characteristic stresses. As we have seen, the Barbie books often depict Barbie guiding her younger sisters and their friends. Several of the Barbie sets convey a sense of this mothering function, and therefore begin to approach the relational model of the Doll House. For instance, even though the dolls in Gardening Fun—Barbie and Kelly are impeccably overdressed, the set nevertheless suggests a joint activity for the sisters that does not revolve around self-fashioning. After all, they are going outside to work together, producing something other than their beautiful selves. With its real-life gardening instructions on the box, the product shifts emphasis for the child in similar ways, directing her focus outward, toward producing rather than consuming. Similarly, the Holiday Sisters (Barbie, Stacie, and Kelly) are dressed for winter festivities (Christmas, Hanukkah, Kwanzaa), but not inappropriately so (as with Birthday Barbie); this set of three dolls again suggests a family affair, a celebration of more than the self. I don't think it is accidental that Skipper, the teen sister, is left out of these rituals.

Meaning shifts in precisely the other direction in one of the few Doll House products to feature a teenager: the Dream Doll House Dress Shop. This set comes with a teen figure; outfits and accessories including a lace skirt, a floral skirt, a denim skirt, a scarf, a boa, and so forth, for her to try on and buy; and a shop, complete with counters and fitting rooms. But as in various Barbie shopping environments, this girl is strangely alone with all her finery—not a village vendor in sight! Despite her comparatively primitive design, this teen figure is indeed a proto-Barbie, inhabiting a world where buying, self-adornment, isolation, and narcissism are the norm. The Dream Doll House Dress Shop shows that whether we're parents, teachers, toy executives, or teenagers, when we think of adolescent girls, it is all too easy to abandon the family values of the Doll House and travel the perilous distance to the Barbie aisle.[22]

If Barbie is a "body project" girl, she is, as others have observed, part of a complex of widespread and destructive messages directed toward women: being tall and thin is crucial, being white is the norm against which others are defined, one's character and career are always less important than one's looks, and consumerism is essential for keeping up appearances. But if I am critical of Barbie as a vessel of ideology, I refuse to condemn her as necessarily harmful for little girls. Or, to be more specific, for those girls who buy her most often and toward whom Mattel primarily directs its marketing: white, middle-class girls. As a white woman, I don't presume to speak for women of color, or to judge what it feels like to see white racial dominance reflected in the world of dolls.

Viewing Barbie as harmful simplifies her complexity. Many writers, while well aware of and even sympathetic to critiques of Barbie, have found other aspects of the doll to be more important than her negative drawbacks. Even if Barbie's message were unilaterally bad, it is not at all clear that all girls, or even most girls, would necessarily internalize a message about body type or identity simply by playing with Barbie. As Yona Zeldis McDonough has argued, there are many other more cogent models than Barbie for girls to follow.[23] Even Barbie's most stringent critics admit the possibility of competing influences.

The assumption that Barbie is harmful also posits a seamlessness between ideology and its reception. In the eighteenth century, critics worried that reading romantic novels would give women flighty ideas about love and deter them from considering eligible suitors. But most women made sensible marriages despite their exposure to novels. I'd worry more about the novels than about Barbie, for surely narrative has more persuasive power than objects—witness our own fear about the connection between violence on television and our violent culture. Moreover, Barbie demands active invention on the part of the child, which provides her with ample opportunity to refashion Barbie's message. The same is true for adults who "play" with Barbie. As Erica Rand has shown, the subversive use of Barbie as a "queer accessory," a fetish of gay and lesbian culture, as well as a cultural icon put to many other uses than those envisioned by Mattel, shows us that Barbie is not merely a tool of dominant patriarchal and misogynistic culture.[24] The fact that Mattel tries regularly to control the appropriation of Barbie's image through lawsuits indicates that Barbie's "message" is not simple—nor is it simply received.

Like so many Barbie critics before me, my analysis turns ultimately from theory to empiricism. It seems that for those of us born in the last forty-five years or so, Barbie has been an important part of our childhood—and how we love to talk about this! And how many of us have a soft spot for her, in spite of ourselves. When I asked a lesbian, feminist friend whether her Barbie collection was at odds with her identity and her politics, she replied, "I played with Barbie all the time as a child and look at how I turned out."[25] A male professor remarked that he has been repeatedly astonished by the strong and positive Barbie nostalgia among women in the largely progressive, largely feminist Cornell community. In the end, despite my own awareness of and distaste for much that Barbie signifies, I don't hate or repudiate her, largely because of my own experience as a Barbie "consumer."

As a mother, I was ambivalent and noncommittal about letting my daughters own Barbie dolls: I wasn't going to introduce them to Barbie, but I would buy them Barbies if they asked for them, and I did not forbid Barbie as a gift. Not surprisingly, my daughter Jocelyn received two Barbies from friends on her sixth birthday: Sweetheart Barbie and Bead Blast Barbie. She completely ignored the beads and the clothes, and was remarkably uninterested in acquiring more of a wardrobe or accessories for her dolls. This remains true; even though she accompanied me several months later to Toys "Я" Us as I researched the line of Barbie products, she did not want to buy anything further. What she did do with her Barbies is construct an intricate and ongoing story, which I will condense as follows: The two Barbies, Michelle and Sara, live together and own a horse named Triumph. Michelle is a veterinarian, and she soon quits her job to stay home and care for the horse (a message to Mom?). Triumph grows up, has a baby, and eventually dies. The Barbies are sad but find solace in raising the new baby horse. At the end of the story, Michelle and Sara marry one another. Now, I grant that my daughter is young and has years to internalize a different message from Barbie, but I was nevertheless astonished at the sheer subversiveness of this narrative vis-à-vis Mattel's intentions. Yet Jocelyn is not unfeminine in the traditional sense of the word. She wears only dresses and she takes pride in her appearance. What her narrative reveals to me is a tremendous exercise of choice and will in her response to cultural signals. I fervently hope that she will retain this power of discrimination as she matures.

I, too, made up stories with my Barbies as a child. Although I can't remember what they were about, I do remember spending hours alone in my room every day playing with Barbie and her various friends. My stories were all-consuming; I remember how annoyed I was at distractions such as homework and chores. And these narratives were ongoing, serialized from day to day, like a soap opera or a novel written in installments. Perhaps this could have happened with other dolls as well—I occasionally played with my international doll collection in a somewhat similar way. But whether it was the realistic nature of the dolls (despite their ludicrous body proportions), or the large gallery of available peers, no toy ever engendered such attention and devotion as my Barbies. Barbie was instrumental in my intensely creative and imaginative inner life.

It was in fact when I stopped playing with Barbie that I got into trouble—in other words, when I entered that perilous time of preadolescence when girls notoriously lose self-esteem. I suppose one could argue that I had absorbed Barbie's harmful message for women and began to feel its effects only when they became relevant to my own life and body. But I suspect that my horrific adolescence had more to do with my entry into female teenage culture. The creative energy that I had funneled into my Barbie play now went to obsessing about my body. I was five-foot-seven and a hundred pounds, but I thought I was fat; I dwelled endlessly on what I did and didn't eat. Each day was a struggle with the body project. I was uncomfortable with my body and uncomfortable with my "self."

It took time and work to repair the ruins of my fall and to find my identity as a teacher and writer. And although I can thankfully say that I've fully recovered from adolescence, I loathe and fear the culture that brings so much pain to so many of our young women. There is also no doubt in my mind that Barbie is symptomatic of that culture. Nevertheless, even as I criticize Barbie at length and in detail, I know that as I write this article, I am drawing on the same part of my brain that invented those Barbie stories years ago. So I remain divided. And hopeful that Barbie will see the light. I long for University Barbie to throw off the cheerleading outfit and put on the workaday jeans and puffy down jacket so necessary for a winter at Cornell. I long for Workin' Out Barbie to play some softball. I long for Birthday Barbie to forget the clothes and enjoy the party. And I long for Talking Barbie to tell Mattel what she really thinks of them for making her a victim of the body project.

or so many of us, the point of Barbie was sex, though we probably couldn't have told you that way back then when we were making her strip and strut. Here, then, is my own homage to the doll who helped me to imagine what went on behind the grown-ups' closed doors.

SEX AND THE SINGLE DOLL

Yona Zeldis McDonough

*N*ow that my son is six and inextricably linked to the grade school social circuit, he gets invited to birthday parties. Lots of them. Whenever I telephone to say he's coming, I always ask for hints on what might be a particularly coveted gift for the birthday child. And whenever that child is a girl, I secretly hope that the answer will be the dirty little word I am longing to hear: *Barbie.*

No such luck. In the liberal Brooklyn neighborhood where we live, there is a definite bias against the poor doll, a veritable Barbie backlash. "My daughter loves her, but I can't stand her," laments one mother. "I won't let her in the house," asserts another. "Oh, please!" sniffs a third.

But I love Barbie. I loved her in 1963, when she first made her entrance into my life. She was blond, with a Jackie Kennedy bouffant hairdo. Her thickly painted lids (carved out of plastic) and pouty, unsmiling mouth gave her a look both knowing and sullen. She belonged to a grown-up world of cocktail dresses, cigarette smoke, and perfume. I loved her in the years that followed, too, when she developed bendable joints; a twist-and-turn waist; long, silky ash-blond hair; and feathery, lifelike eyelashes. I never stopped loving her. I never will.

I've heard all the arguments against her: She's a bimbo and an airhead; she's an insatiable consumer—for tarty clothes, a dream house filled with garish pink furniture, a pink Barbie-mobile—who teaches little girls that there is nothing in life quite so exciting as shopping. Her body, with its buoyant breasts, wasplike waist, and endless legs defies all human proportion. But at six, I inchoately understood Barbie's appeal: pure sex. My other dolls were either babies or little girls, with flat chests and chubby legs. Even the other so-called fashion dolls—Tammy, in her aqua-and-white playsuit, and Tressy, with that useless hank of hair, couldn't compete. Barbie was clearly a woman doll, and a woman was what I longed to be.

When I was eight, and had just learned about menstruation, I fashioned a small sanitary napkin for her out of neatly folded tissues. Rubber bands held it in place. "Oh, look," said my bemused mother, "Barbie's got her little period. Now she can have a baby." I was disappointed, but my girlfriends all snickered in a much more satisfying way. You see, I wanted Barbie to be, well, dirty. We all did.

Our Barbies had sex, at least our childish version of it. They hugged and kissed the few available boy dolls we had—clean-cut and oh-so-square Ken, the more relaxed and sexy Allan. They also danced, pranced, and strutted, but mostly they stripped, showing off their amazing, no-way-in-the-world human bodies. An adult friend tells me how she used to put her Barbie's low-backed bathing suit on backwards so the doll's breasts were exposed. I liked dressing mine in her pink-and-white candy-striped baby-sitter's apron—and nothing else.

I've also heard that Barbie is a poor role model for little girls. Is there such widespread contempt for the intelligence of children that we really imagine they are stupid enough to be shaped by a doll? Girls learn how to be women not from their dolls but from the women around them. Most often this means Mom.

My own was a march-to-a-different-drummer bohemian in the early sixties. She eschewed the beauty parlor, cards, and mah-jongg that the other moms in the neighborhood favored. Instead, she wore her long black hair loose, her earrings big and dangling, and her lipstick dark. She made me a Paris bistro birthday party with candles stuck in old wine bottles, red-and-white-checked tablecloths for decorations; she read the poetry of T. S. Eliot to the assembled group of enchanted ten-year-olds. She was, in those years, an aspiring painter, and her work graced not only the walls of our apartment, but also the shower curtain, bathroom mirror, and a chest of drawers in my room. She—not an eleven-and-half-a-inch doll—was the most powerful female role model in my life. What she thought of Barbie I really don't know, but she had the good sense to back off and let me use the doll in my own way.

Barbie has become more politically correct over the years. She no longer looks so vixenish, and has traded the sultry expression I remember for one that is more wholesome and less covert. She now exists in a variety of "serious" incarnations: teacher, Olympic athlete, dentist. And Mattel recently introduced the Really Rad Barbie, a doll whose breasts and hips are smaller and whose waist is thicker, thus reflecting a more real (as if children wanted their toys to be real) female body. None of this matters one iota. Girls will still know the real reason they love her—and it has nothing to do with new professions or a subtly amended figure.

Fortunately, my Barbie love will no longer have to content itself with buying gifts for my son's friends and the daughters of my own. I have a daughter now, and although she is just two, she already has half a dozen Barbies.

They are, along with various articles of clothing, furniture, and other essential accoutrements, packed away like so many sleeping princesses in translucent pink plastic boxes that line my basement shelves. But the magic for which they wait is no longer the prince's gentle kiss. Instead, it is the heart and mind of my little girl as she picks them up and begins to play. I can hardly wait.

HAPPY BIRTHDAY TO YOU!

Anna Quindlen is no fan of Barbie; she wouldn't let her daughter own one, no matter how loud the whining and pleading got. Nevertheless, she was moved to convey her personal birthday wishes to Barbie five years ago, on the occasion of the doll's thirty-fifth birthday. Here is her birthday message to Barbie, reprinted from The New York Times.

Comic writer Susan Shapiro has also written a birthday greeting to Barbie. In her essay, reprinted here from The New York Times Magazine, *she credits the doll with having taught her some essential "life lessons."*

BARBIE AT 35

Anna Quindlen

$\mathcal{M}$y theory is that to get rid of Barbie you'd have to drive a silver stake through her plastic heart. Or a silver lamé stake, the sort of thing that might accompany Barbie's Dream Tent.

This is not simply because the original Barbie, launched lo these thirty-five years ago, was more than a little vampiric in appearance, more Natasha of *Rocky and Bullwinkle* than the "ultimate girl next door" Mattel describes in her press kit.

It's not only that Barbie, like Dracula, can appear in guises that mask her essential nature: surgeon, astronaut, Unicef ambassador. Or that she is untouched by time, still that same parody of the female form she's been since 1959. She's said by her manufacturers to be "eleven and one-half stylish inches" tall. If she were a real-live woman she would not have enough body fat to menstruate regularly. Which may be why there's no PMS Barbie.

The silver stake is necessary because Barbie—the issue, not the doll—simply will not be put to rest.

"Mama, why can't I have Barbie?"

"Because I hate Barbie. She gives little girls the message that the only thing that's important is being tall and thin and having a big chest and lots of clothes. She's a terrible role model."

"Oh, Mama, don't be silly. She's just a toy."

It's an excellent comeback; if only it were accurate. But consider the recent study at the University of Arizona investigating the attitudes of white and black teenage girls toward body image.

The attitudes of the white girls were a nightmare. Ninety percent expressed dissatisfaction with their own bodies and many said they saw dieting as a kind of all-purpose panacea. "I think the reason I would diet would be to gain self-confidence," said one. "I'd feel like it was a way of getting control," said another.

And they were curiously united in their description of the perfect girl. She's five feet seven inches, weighs just over a hundred pounds, has long legs and flowing hair. The researchers concluded, "The ideal girl was a living manifestation of the Barbie doll."

While the white girls described an impossible ideal, black teenagers talked about appearance in terms of style, attitude, pride, and personality. White respondents talked "thin," black ones "shapely." Seventy percent of the black teenagers said they were satisfied with their weight, and there was little emphasis on dieting. "We're all brought up and taught to be realistic about life," said one, "and we don't look at things the way you want them to be. You look at them the way they are."

There's a quiet irony in that. While black women correctly complain that they are not sufficiently represented in advertisements, commercials, movies, even dolls, perhaps the scarcity of those idealized and unrealistic models may help in some fashion to liberate black teenagers from ridiculous standards of appearance. When the black teenagers were asked about the ideal woman, many asked: Whose ideal? The perfect girl projected by the white world simply didn't apply to them or their community, which set beauty standards from within. "White girls," one black participant in the Arizona study wrote, "have to look like Barbie dolls."

There are lots of reasons teenage girls have such a distorted fun house—mirror image of their own bodies, so distorted that one study found that 83 percent wanted to lose weight, although 62 percent were in the normal range. Fashion designers still showcase anorexia chic; last year the supermodel Kate Moss was reduced to insisting that, yes, she did eat.

But long before Kate and Ultra Slimfast came along, hanging over the lives of every little girl born in the second half of the twentieth century was the impossibly curvy shadow (40-18-32 in life-size terms) of Barbie. That preposterous physique, we learn as kids, is what a woman looks like with her clothes off. "Two Barbie dolls are sold every second," says Barbie's résumé, which is more extensive than that of Hillary Rodham Clinton. "Barbie doll has had more than a billion pairs of shoes . . . has had over 500 professional makeovers . . . has become the most popular toy ever created."

Has been single-handedly responsible for the popularity of the silicone implant?

Maybe, as my daughter suggests while she whines in her Barbie-free zone, that's too much weight to put on something that's just a toy. Maybe not. Happy birthday, Babs. Have a piece of cake. Have two.

MY MENTOR, BARBIE

Susan Shapiro

Instead of throwing Barbie a thirty-fifth birthday party, feminists have been dissing the popular, petite plaything. Yet far from being a bad role model, Barbie could be a modern girl's dream mentor. OK, so she does have the equivalent of a sixteen-inch waist. Over the years, I still learned some very important life lessons from Barbie.

1. *Family Is Fundamental:* Barbie's my age and, as the long-awaited only girl in a suburban clan of boys, I was Mattel's dream customer. I had sixty-eight Barbies who shared a pink plastic convertible car and split-level condominium, along with twelve Little Kiddies and twenty-eight Dawn dolls so tiny that instead of changing their clothes I just switched their heads.

2. *Many Girls Have the Same Name:* There were six Susans in my second-grade class, which caused two of them, on the first day of school, to run home crying. Not me—I'd spent my formative years with Talking Barbie, Tropical Barbie, Color Magic Barbie,

Twist 'n Turn Barbie, Living Barbie, and three Malibu Barbies, which taught me that individuality was determined not by your name but by what special activities you did best.

3. *A Shortage of Men Won't Ruin the Party:* Whether it was an elaborate prom spread out on the pink carpet or a Barbie beach holiday (where I locked myself in the bathroom and hurled them headfirst into the sink), the guest list always read: red-headed Barbie, Malibu Barbie triplets, cousin Francie, Scooter, Skipper, Casey, Christie, Julia, Stacey (visiting from England), Midge, Dawn, Angie, Twiggy, Ken. I heard there was a Ricky, but I could never find him. I did steal my brother's G.I. Joe. But since my father was a doctor, G.I. Joe became an army surgeon who returned from a long day at the base hospital screaming: "I just saved nine people from fatal heart attacks and you expect me to go to a party later? Don't you women know I'm exhausted?" Thus I realized, way back then, that women have superior social etiquette and most important galas do not require the attendance of guys.

4. *Alternative Lifestyles Are Acceptable:* In a doll domain with ninety-six eligible females and Ken, unusual pairings were common. Sometimes Skipper and Scooter slept in the guest room shoe box with Casey. One night I found the Malibu Barbie trio in my desk drawer on top of cousin Francie. It was OK by me— as long as they followed one rule: Everyone shares clothes. And since afternoon teas and disco dances were hard to attend if you had a child to look after, each Little Kiddie was assigned nine mothers, who rotated child-care responsibilities.

5. *It's Cool to Have Many Careers:* At different stages, Barbie was a ballerina, torch singer, equestrienne, majorette, stewardess, astronaut with pink space-pants outfit, nurse, doctor, and fashion model, which paved the way for my subsequent employment as receptionist, poet, secretary, paperback-book critic, waitress, and part-time teacher.

6. *You Can Have Love and Work at the Same Time:* Throughout Barbie's professional soul-searching, Ken was a constant. He didn't question why she needed fulfillment outside the home. When she went Malibu, he got tan, too. When she was Guinevere, he was secure enough in his masculinity to wear a silver lamé tunic, footed pants, and gold belt with his scabbard and sword.

7. *Dysfunction and Deformity Are a Part of Life:* In a full day of playing in a pink-flowered room, accidents were bound to happen. The pink convertible kept crashing into the pink stereo, and once, I stashed Midge in my Suzy Homemaker oven, but G.I. Joe rescued her right before meltdown. Another time, redheaded Barbie wound up with half her nose and hair cut off, hanging from the pull chain of the light in my bedroom. But burned, squashed, or decapitated, they were still included in all cookouts, coed classes, or slumber parties.

8. *War Is Hell:* Despite repeated warnings from my (redheaded) mother, many an after-school social was marred by attacks from my brothers and their snake, spider, and battalions of little green army men. We were always on alert because any minute, they could bomb us with water balloon grenades or Lucky Charms. After each battle, it took days to get everything back in working order and for calm to be restored.

9. *All Homeless Must Be Sheltered:* When in need, emergency sleeping arrangements called for boot-box extra bedrooms, filled with my mother's sanitary-napkin cots and high heels doubling as bunk beds. Room was always made for such transients as my cousin Lisa's Chatty Cathy, my neighbor Jill's orange and purple alien trolls (visiting from another planet), and several dozen little green P.O.W.s.

10. *Monogamy Can Work:* Once she and Ken tied the knot, Barbie did not play around. OK, Ken didn't have much competition,

although Barbie was once tempted by the romantic antics of G.I. Joe, who could twist his arms and legs around in a complete circle. He had a fling with Francie instead, and Barbie wound up back with dependable Ken. When he got on her nerves—she just tossed him under the bed.

Parents, scholars, and educators have noticed and commented upon the incredible whiteness of Barbie, and the way in which her inexorably blond, fairskinned image can undermine the self-esteem of little girls of color. Over the years, Mattel has attempted to address these concerns by adding several AfricanAmerican dolls to the Barbie family tree. Despite this nod to cultural difference, scholar Ann duCille maintains that the doll's message nonetheless stresses conformity and homogeny above all. This essay is excerpted from a longer chapter in her book Skin Trade, *which deals with gender as well as race. The selection here, however, focuses on the subtle interplay between race and power that dominates the many characters in Barbie land.*

BARBIE IN BLACK
AND WHITE

Ann duCille

In today's toy world, race and ethnicity have fallen into the category of precious ready-to-wear difference. To be profitable, racial and cultural diversity—global heterogeneity—must be reducible to such common, reproducible denominators as color and costume. Race and racial differences—whatever that might mean in the grander social order—must be reducible to skin color or, more correctly, to the tint of the plastic poured into each Barbie mold. Each doll is marketed as representing something or someone in the real world, even as the political, social, and economic particulars of that world are not only erased but, in a curious way, made the same. Black Jamaican Barbie—outfitted as a peasant or a maid—stands alongside white English Barbie, who is dressed in the fancy riding habit of a lady of leisure. On the toy-store shelf or in the collector's curio cabinet, maid and aristocrat enjoy an odd equality (they even sell for the same price), but this seeming sameness denies the historical relation they bear to each other as the colonized and the colonizer.

If we could line up the ninety or so different colors, cultures, and other incarnations in which Barbie currently exits, the physical facts of her unrelenting sameness (or at least similarity) would become immediately apparent. Even two dolls might do the trick: white Western Fun Barbie and black Western Fun Barbie, for example. Except for their dye jobs, the dolls are identical: the same body, size, shape, and apparel. Or perhaps I should say *nearly* identical, because in some instances—with black and Asian dolls in particular—coloring and other subtle changes (slanted eyes in the Asian dolls, thicker lips in the black dolls) suggest differently coded facial features.

In other instances, when Barbie moves across cultural as opposed to racial lines, it is costume rather than color that distinguishes one ethnic group or nation from another. Nigeria and Jamaica, for instance, are represented by the same basic brown body and face mold, dolled up in different native garbs, or Mattel's interpretation thereof.[1] With other costume changes, this generic black body and face can be Marine Barbie or Army Barbie or even Presidential Candidate Barbie. Much the same is true of the generic Asian doll—sometimes called Kira—who reappears in a variety of different dress-defined ethnicities. In other words, where Barbie is concerned, clothes not only make the woman, they mark the racial and/or cultural difference.

Such difference is marked as well by the miniature cultural history and language lessons that accompany each doll in Mattel's international collection. The back of Jamaican Barbie's box tells us: "*How-you-du* (Hello) from the land of Jamaica, a tropical paradise known for its exotic fruit, sugarcane, breathtaking beaches, and reggae beat!" In an odd rendering of cause and effect, the box goes on to explain that "most Jamaicans have ancestors from Africa, so even though our official language is English, we speak patois, a kind of '*Jamaica Talk*,' filled with English and African words.[2] For example, when I'm filled with *boonoonoonoos*, I'm filled with much happiness!" So written, Jamaica becomes an exotic tropical isle where happy,

FIGURE 1
Barbie in Original Swimsuit, 1959.
Private Collection.

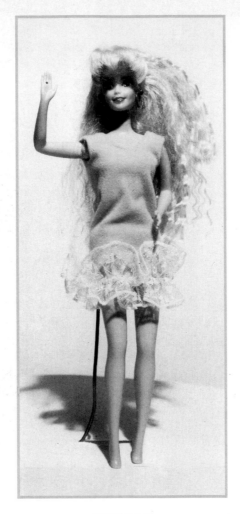

FIGURE 2
Barbie, 1991. Collection Sophia Grudin.

PHOTO: LE CLAIRE CUSTOM COLOR

FIGURE 3
Barbie and Ken Undressed, 1991.
Collection Sophia Grudin.
PHOTO: LE CLAIRE CUSTOM COLOR

FIGURE 4
William Bouguereau,
The Birth of Venus, 1879. Oil on canvas.
Musée d'Orsay, Paris.

(R.M.N.)

FIGURE 5
Michelangelo Buonarroti, *David.*
Accademia, Florence.

FIGURE 6

Bild Lilli cartoon, 1950s.

COPYRIGHT *BILD ZEITUNG*

FIGURE 7
Maggie Robbins,
Barbie Fetish, 1989.

PHOTO: CAROLINA SALGUERO

FIGURE 8
Cindy Sherman, *Untitled #255,*
1992. Color photograph.

COURTESY OF METRO PICTURES, NEW YORK

FIGURE 9
Barbie in pose of Cindy
Sherman's *Untitled #255,* 1992.

PHOTO: LE CLAIRE CUSTOM COLOR

dark-skinned, English-speaking peasants don't really speak English.

Presented as if out of the mouths of native informants, the cultural captions on the boxes help to sell the impression that what we see isn't all we get with these dolls. The use of first-person narration lends a stamp of approval and a voice of authority to the object, confirming that the consumer has purchased not only a toy or a collector's item to display but access to another culture, inside knowledge of an exotic, foreign other. The invariably cheerful greetings and the warm, chatty tone affirm that all's well with the small world. As a marketing strategy, these captions contribute to the museum of culture effect, but as points of information, such reductive ethnographies only enhance the extent to which these would-be multicultural dolls make race and ethnicity collectors' items, contributing more to the stock exchange than to cultural exchange.

$\mathcal{N}$ot entirely immune to criticism of its identity politics, Mattel sought advice from black parents and specialists in early-childhood development in the making and marketing of a new assortment of black Barbie dolls—the Shani line. Chief among the expert witnesses was the clinical psychologist Darlene Powell Hopson, who coauthored with her husband, Derek Hopson, a study of racism and child development, *Different and Wonderful: Raising Black Children in a Race-Conscious Society* (1990). As part of their research and clinical work, the Hopsons repeated a ground-breaking study conducted by the black psychologists Kenneth and Mamie Clark in the 1940s.

The Clarks used dolls to demonstrate the negative effects of racism and segregation on black children. When given a choice between a white doll and a black doll, nearly 70 percent of the black children in the study chose the white doll. The Clarks' findings became an important factor in *Brown v. Board of Education* in 1954. More recently, scholars have called into question both

the Clarks' methodology and the meaning ascribed to their findings: the assumption that a black child's choosing a white doll
necessarily reflects a negative self-concept.[3] William Cross has
argued, for example, that the Clarks confounded two different
issues: attitude toward race in general and attitude toward the
self in particular. How one feels about race or what one knows
of societal attitudes toward the racially marked is not always an
index of one's own self-esteem; or, as Harriette Pipes McAdoo
suggests, perhaps black children "are able to compartmentalize
their view of themselves from their view of their racial group."[4]

Such qualifications—coupled with the evidence of my own
experience (my dreaming through a white male persona as a
child did not mean that I hated my black female self)—have
also led me to question the Clark studies. For Darlene and
Derek Hopson, however, the research remains compelling. In
1985 they repeated the Clarks' doll test and found that 65 percent of the black children in their sample chose a white doll over
a black one. Moreover, 76 percent of the children interviewed
said that the black dolls looked "bad" to them. Based on their
own doll tests and their clinical work with children, the Hopsons concluded that black children, "in great numbers," continue to identify with white images—even when black images
are made available. "Our empirical results confirmed the messages Black children were sending us every day in our practice,"
the Hopsons explain. "We're not as good, as pretty, or as nice as
Whites. . . . We don't like being Black. We wish we could be like
them."[5]

The Hopson findings sent shock waves across the country
and around the world. The interest their results generated among
social scientists, parents, and the popular press prompted the
Hopsons to write *Different and Wonderful*, a guidebook in which
they use their experience as psychologists and as parents to suggest ways of counteracting negative racialized imagery. Several
of their interventional strategies involve "doll play," and here
again the ubiquitous Barbie has a featured role.

"If your daughter likes 'Barbie' dolls, by all means get her

Barbie," the Hopsons advise black parents. "*But also* choose Black characters from the Barbie world."[6] Admittedly, I know more about word usage than about child psychology, but it seems to me that the Hopsons' own phrasing may speak to at least one problem with their positive play methodology and the role of Barbie in it. "Barbie," unmodified in the preceding statement, apparently means *white* Barbie, suggesting that the Hopsons also take white Barbie dolls as the norm. Black Barbie is toyland's "but also," just as black people are society's "but also."

The problem here is not simply semantic. Barbie has a clearly established persona and a thoroughly pervasive presence as a white living doll. The signature Barbies, the dolls featured on billboards, on boxes, in video and board games, on clothing, and in the Barbie exercise tape (as well as the actresses who play Barbie on Broadway and the models who make special appearances as Barbie at Disneyland and elsewhere) are always blond, blue-eyed, and white. Colorizing Barbie, selling her in blackface, does not necessarily make her over into a positive black image.

"My daughter wants to know why she can't have a white Barbie doll," one African-American mother told me. "She's been playing happily with black Barbie dolls since she was two, but lately she wants to know why she can't have a white doll; why she can't have the *real Barbie.*" The four-year-old's words, like the Hopsons' "but also," speak to the larger color biases of imagery, texts, and toys that persist more than fifty years after the Clark study. If black children continue to identify with white images, it may be because even the would-be positive black images around them—including black Barbie dolls—serve to reinforce their second-class citizenship.[7]

But there may be other problems with the well-meaning advice offered black parents in *Different and Wonderful.* The Hopsons suggest that parents should not only provide their children with ethnic dolls, but that they also should get involved in the doll play. "Help them dress and groom the dolls while you compliment them both," they advise, offering this routine: "This is a beautiful doll. It looks just like you. Look at her hair. It's just like yours. Did you know your nose is as pretty as your doll's?" They further recommend that parents use "complimentary words such as *lovely, pretty,* or *nice* so that [the] child will learn to associate them with his or her own image."[8]

Certainly it is important to help black children feel good about themselves, which includes helping them to be comfortable with their own bodies. One might argue, however, that these suggestions run the risk of transmitting to the black child a colorized version of the same old white beauty myth. Like Barbie dolls themselves, these techniques for positive play not only make beauty a desirable fixed physical fact—a matter of characteristics rather than character—they make this embodied beauty synonymous with self-worth. A better strategy might be to use the doll to show children how *unlike* any real woman Barbie is. In spite of their own good intentions, the Hopsons in effect have endorsed the same bill of goods Mattel has made the basis of its ethnically oriented marketing campaign—a campaign launched perhaps not entirely coincidentally in the fall of 1991, the year after the Hopsons' book *Different and Wonderful* appeared.

Though one can only speculate about a link between the publication of *Different and Wonderful* and Mattel's going ethnic in its advertising, it is clear that the Hopsons' strategies for using dolls to instill ethnic pride caught the company's attention.[9] In 1990, Darlene Hopson was asked to consult with Mattel's product manager Deborah Mitchell and designer Kitty Black Perkins—both African Americans—in the development of a new line of "realistically sculpted" black fashion dolls. Hopson agreed, and about a year later Shani and her friends Asha and Nichelle became the newest members of Barbie's entourage.

According to the doll's package:

Shani means marvelous in the Swahili language . . . and marvelous she is! With her friends Asha and Nichelle, Shani brings to life the special style and beauty of the African American woman. Each one is beautiful in her own way, with her own lovely skin shade and unique facial features. Each has a different hair color and texture, perfect for braiding, twisting and creating fabulous hair styles! Their clothes, too, reflect the vivid colors and ethnic accents that showcase their exotic looks and fashion flair![10]

These words attempt to convey a message of black pride—after the fashion of the Hopsons' recommendations for positive play—but that message is clearly tied to bountiful hair, lavish and exotic clothes, and other external signs of beauty, wealth, and success.

Mattel gave Shani a coming-out party at the International Toy Fair in February 1991. Also making their debuts were Shani's friends Asha and Nichelle, notable for the different hues in which their black plastic skin comes—an innovation due in part to Darlene Hopson. Shani, the signature doll of the line, is what some would call brown-skinned; Asha is honey-colored; and Nichelle is deep mahogany. Their male friend, Jamal, added in 1992, completes the collection.

The three-to-one ratio of the Shani quartet—three black females to one black male—may be the most realistic thing about these dolls. In the eyes of Mattel, however, Shani and her friends are the most authentic black dolls yet produced in the mainstream toy market. Billed as "Tomorrow's African American woman," Shani has broader hips, fuller lips, and a broader nose, according to Deborah Mitchell. Kitty Black Perkins, who has dressed black Barbies since their birth in 1980, adds that the Shani dolls are also distinguished by their unique, culturally specific clothes in "spice tones, [and] ethnic fabrics," rather than "fantasy colors like pink or lavender"[11]—evidently the colors of the faint of skin.

The notion that fuller lips, broader noses, wider hips, and higher derrieres make the Shani dolls more realistically African-American again raises many difficult questions about difference, authenticity, and the problematic categories of the real and the symbolic, the typical and the stereotypical. Again we have to ask what authentic blackness looks like. Even if we knew, how could this ethnic or racial authenticity ever be achieved in a doll? Also, where capital is concerned, the profit motive must always intersect with all other incentives.

The Shani doll is an apt illustration of this point. On the one hand, Mattel was concerned enough about producing a more "ethnically correct" black doll to seek the advice of black image specialists in the development and marketing of the Shani line. On the other hand, the company was not willing to follow the advice of such experts where doing so would entail a retooling that would cost the corporation more than the price of additional dyes and fabrics.

For example, Darlene Hopson argued not just for gradations in skin tones in the Shani dolls, but also for variations in body type and hair styles. But, while Mattel acknowledged both the legitimacy and the ubiquity of such arguments, the ever-present profit incentive militated against breaking the mold, even for the sake of the illusion of realism. "To be truly realistic, one [Shani doll] should have shorter hair," Deborah Mitchell has admitted. "But little girls of all races love hair play. We added more texture. But we can't change the fact that long, combable hair is still a key seller."

In fact, there have been a number of times when Mattel has changed the length and style of its dolls' hair. Christie, the black doll that replaced Colored Francie in 1968, had a short Afro, which was more in keeping with what was perhaps the signature black hairstyle of the sixties. Other shorter styles have appeared as the fashions of the moment dictated. In the early sixties, Barbie sported a bubble cut like Jacqueline Kennedy's.[12] Today, though, Mattel seems less willing to crop Barbie's hair in accord with fashion. Donna Gibbs, media-relations director at Mattel, told me that the long hair of Mattel's dolls is the result of research into play patterns. "Combing, cutting, and styling hair is basic to the play patterns of girls of all ethnicities," she said. All of the products are test-marketed first with both children and adults, and the designs are based on such research.[13]

Hair play is no doubt a favorite pastime with little girls. But Mattel, I would argue, doesn't simply respond to the desire among girls for dolls with long hair to comb; it helps to produce those desires. Most Barbie dolls come with a little comb or brush, and ads frequently show girls brushing, combing, and braiding their dolls' long hair. In recent years, Mattel has taken its invitation to hair play to new extremes with its mass production of Totally Hair Barbie. Hollywood Hair Barbie. and Cut and Style Barbie—dolls whose Rapunzel-like hair lets down in seemingly endless locks. (Cut and Style Barbie comes with "functional sharp edge" scissors and an extra wad of attachable hair. Hair refill packs are sold separately.) But what does the transference of flowing fairy-princess hair onto black dolls mean for the black children for whom these dolls are supposed to inspire self-esteem?

In the process of my own archival research—poking around in the dusty aisles of Toys "Я" Us—I encountered a black teenage girl in search of the latest black Barbie. During the impromptu interview that ensued, my subject confessed to me in graphic detail the many Barbie murders and mutilations she had committed over the years. "It's the hair," she said emphatically several times. "The hair, that hair; I want it. I want it!" Her words recalled my own torturous childhood struggles with the straightening combs, curling irons, and chemical relaxers that biweekly transformed my woolly "just like a sponge" kinks into what the white kids at school marveled at as my "Cleopatra [straight] hair."

Many African-American women and quite a few African-American men have similar tales about dealing with their hair or with the hair of daughters or sisters or mothers. In "Life with Daughters," the black essayist Gerald Early recounts the difficulties that arose when Linnet, the elder of his two daughters, decided that she wanted hair that would "blow in the wind," while at the same time neither she nor her mother wanted her to have her hair straightened. "I do not think Linnet wanted to change her hair to be beautiful," Early writes; "she wanted to be like everyone else. But perhaps this is simply wishful thinking here or playing with words, because Linnet must have felt her difference as being a kind of ugliness."[14]

Indeed, "colored hair," like dark skin, has been both culturally and commercially constructed as ugly, nappy, wild, and woolly, in constant need of taming, straightening, cropping, and cultivating.[15] In the face of such historically charged constructions, it is difficult for black children not to read their hair as different and that difference as ugly. Stories and pictures abound of little black girls putting towels on their heads and pretending that the towels are long hair that can blow in the wind or be tossed over the shoulder. But ambivalence about or antipathy toward the hair on our heads is hardly limited to the young. Adult African Americans spend millions each year on a variety of products that promise to straighten, relax, or otherwise make more manageable kinky black hair.[16] And who can forget the painful scene—made hilarious by Spike Lee and Denzel Washington in *Malcolm X*—in which his friend Shorty gives the young Malcolm Little his first conk?

Mattel may have a point. It may be that part of Shani's and black Barbie's attraction for little black girls—as for all children and perhaps even for adults—is the dolls' fairy-princess good looks, the crowning touch of glory of which is long, straight hair, combable locks that cascade down the dolls' backs. Even though it is not as easy to comb as Mattel maintains, for black girls the simulated hair on the heads of Shani and black Barbie may suggest more than simple hair play; it may represent a fanciful alternative to what society presents as their own less-attractive, short, kinky, hurts-to-comb hair.

As difficult as this prospect is to consider, its ancillary implications are even more jarring. If Colored Francie failed in 1967 partly because of her "Caucasian features" and her long, straight hair, is Shani such a success in the 1990s because of those same features? Is the popularity of these thin-bodied, straight-haired dolls a sign that black is most beautiful when readable in traditional white terms? Have blacks, too, bought the dominant ideals of beauty inscribed in Barbie's svelte figure and flowing locks?

It would be difficult to answer these questions, I suppose, without making the kinds of reductive value judgments about the politics of black hair that Kobena Mercer has warned us against: the assumption that "hair styles which avoid artifice and look 'natural,' such as the Afro or Dreadlocks, are the more authentically black hair styles and thus more ideologically 'right-on.'"[17] Suffice it to say that Barbie's svelte figure—like her long hair—became Shani's body type as well, even as Mattel claims to have done the impossible, even as they profess to have captured in this new doll the "unique facial features" and the "special style and beauty of the African American people." This claim seems to be based on subtle changes in the doll that apparently are meant to signify Shani's black difference. Chief among these changes—especially in Soul Train Shani, a scantily clad hip-hop edition of the series released in 1993—is the *illusion* of broader hips and elevated buttocks.

This illusion is achieved by a technological sleight of design that no doubt costs the company far less than all the talk about Shani's broader hips and higher derriere would suggest. No matter what Mattel spokespersons say, Shani—who has to be able to wear Barbie's clothes—is not larger or broader across the hips and behind than other Barbie dolls. In fact, according to the anthropologists Jacqueline Urla and Alan Swedlund, who have studied the anthropometry (body measurements) of Barbie, Shani's seemingly wider hips are if anything a fraction smaller in both circumference and breadth than those of other Barbie dolls. The effect of a higher buttocks is achieved by a change in the angle of the doll's back.[18]

On closer examination, one finds that not only is Shani's back arched, but her legs are also bent in and backward. When laid face down, other Barbie dolls lie flat, but the legs of Soul

Train Shani rise slightly upward. This barely noticeable backward thrust of the legs also enhances the impression of protruding buttocks, the technical term for which is *steatopygia*, defined as an excessive accumulation of fat on the buttocks. (The same technique was used in nineteenth-century art and photography in an attempt to make subjects look more primitive.) Shani's buttocks may appear to protrude, but actually the doll has no posterior deposits of plastic fat and is not dimensionally larger or broader than all the other eleven-and-a-half-inch fashion dolls sold by Mattel. One might say that reports of Shani's butt enhancement have been greatly exaggerated. Her signifying black difference is really just more (or less) of the same.

There is a far more important point to be made, however. Illusion or not, Shani's buttocks can pass for uniquely black only if we accept the stereotypical notion of what blacks look like. Social scientists, historians, literary scholars, and cultural theorists have long argued that race is socially constructed rather than biologically determined. Yet, however coded, notions of race remain finely connected to the biological, the phenotypical, and the physiological in discussions about the racially marked body, not to mention the racially marketed body.

No matter how much scholars attempt to intellectualize it otherwise, *race* generally means "nonwhite," and *black* is still related to skin color, hair texture, facial features, body type, and other outward signifiers of difference. A less neutral term for such signifiers is, of course, *stereotypes*. In playing the game of difference with its ethnic dolls. Mattel either defies or deploys these stereotypes, depending on cost and convenience. "Black hair" might be easy enough to simulate (as in Kenyan Barbie's Astroturf Afro), but—if we buy what Mattel says about its market research—anything other than long straight hair could cost the company some of its young consumers. Mechanical manipulation of Shani's plastic body, on the other hand, represents a facile deployment of stereotype in the service of capital. A *trompe l'oeil* derriere and a dye job transform the already stereotypical white archetype into the black stereotype—into what one might call the Hottentot Venus of toyland.

Indeed, in identifying buttocks as the signifier of black female difference, Mattel may unwittingly be taking us back to the eugenics and scientific racism of earlier centuries. One of the most notorious manifestations of this racism was the use and abuse of so-called Hottentot women such as Sarah Bartmann, whom science and medicine identified as the essence of black female sexuality. Presented to European audiences as the "Hottentot Venus," Saarjie, or Sarah, Bartmann was a young African woman whose large buttocks (common among the people of southern Africa whom Dutch explorers called Hottentots or Bushmen) made her an object of sexual curiosity for white Westerners traveling in Africa. According to Sander Gilman, for Victorians the protruding buttocks of these African women pointed to "the other, hidden sexual signs, both physical and temperamental, of the black female." "Female sexuality is linked to the image of the buttocks," Gilman writes, "and the quintessential buttocks are those of the Hottentot."[19]

Transformed from individual to icon, Bartmann was taken from Cape Town in the early 1800s and widely exhibited before paying audiences in Paris and London between 1810 and her death in 1815 at age twenty-five. According to some accounts, she was made to appear onstage in a manner that confirmed her as the primitive beast she and her people were believed to be. Bartmann's body, which had been such a curiosity during her life, was dissected after her death, her genitals removed, preserved under a bell jar, and placed on display at the Musée de l'Homme in Paris.[20] But as Anne Fausto-Sterling has argued so persuasively, even attempting to tell the known details of the exploitation of this woman, whose given African name is not known, only extends her victimization in the service of intellectual inquiry. The case of Sarah Bartmann, Fausto-Sterling points out, can tell us nothing about the women herself; it can only give us insight into the minds and methodologies of the scientists who made her their subject.[21]

Given this history, it is ironic that Shani's would-be protruding buttocks (even as a false bottom) should be identified as the site and signifier of black female alterity—of "butt also" difference, if I may be pardoned the pun. Georges Cuvier, one of several nineteenth-century scientists to dissect and to write about Bartmann, maintained that the black female "looks different"; her physiognomy, her skin color, and her genitalia mark her as "inherently different."[22] Long since recognized as morbidly racist, the language of Cuvier's "diagnosis" nevertheless resembles the terms in which racial difference is still written today. The problems that underpin Mattel's deep play with Shani's buttocks, then, are the very problems that reside within the grammar of difference in contemporary critical and cultural theory.

With Shani and its other black Barbie dolls, Mattel has made blackness simultaneously visible and invisible, at once different and the same. What Mattel has done with Barbie is not at all unlike what society has done with the facts and fictions of difference over the course of several centuries. In theoretical terms, what's at stake in studying Barbie is much more than just fun and games. In fact, in its play with racial and ethnic alterity, Mattel may well have given us a prism through which to see in living color the degree to which difference is an impossible space—antimatter located not only beyond the grasp of low culture but also beyond the reach of high theory.

Just as Barbie reigns ubiquitously white, blond, and blue-eyed over a rainbow coalition of colored optical illusions, human social relations remain in hierarchical bondage, one to the other, the dominant to the different. Difference is always relational and value-laden. We are not just *different*; we are always *different from*. All theories of difference—from Saussure and Derrida to Fanon and Foucault—are bound by this problematic of relativity. More significantly, all notions of human diversity necessarily constitute difference as oppositional. From the prurient nineteenth-century racism that placed Sarah Bartmann's genitals under a bell jar, to the contemporary IQ-based social Darwinism that places blacks at the bottom of a bell curve, difference is always stacked up against a (superior) center. This is the irony of deconstruction and its failure: things fall apart, but the center holds remarkably firm. It holds precisely because the very act of theorizing difference affirms that there is a center, a standard, or—as in the case of Barbie—a mold.

Yet, however deep its fissures, deconstruction—rather than destruction—may be the closest we can come to a solution to the problem for which Barbie is but one name. Barbie, like racism (if not race), is indestructible. Not even Anna Quindlen's silver-lamé stake through the doll's plastic heart would rid us of this immovable object, which is destined to outlive even its most tenacious critics. (This is literally true, since Barbie dolls are not biodegradable. Remembering the revenge the faithful took on Nietzsche—" 'God is dead,' signed Nietzsche" / " 'Nietzsche is dead,' signed God"—I can see my obituary in *Barbie Bazaar*: " 'duCille is dead,' signed Barbie.") But if, as Wordsworth wrote, we murder to dissect, deconstructing Barbie may be our only release from the doll's impenetrable plastic jaws, just as deconstructing race and gender may be the only way out of the deep space or muddy waters of difference.

The particulars of black Barbie illustrate the difficulties and dangers of treating race and gender differences as biological stigmata that can be fixed in plastic and mass-produced. But if difference is indeed an impossible space—a kind of black hole, if you will—it is antimatter that continues to matter tremendously, especially for those whose bodies bear its visible markings and carry its material consequences.

The answer, then, to the problematic of difference cannot be, as some have argued, that gender does not exist or that race is an empty category. Such arguments throw the body out with the murky bath water. But, as black Barbie and Shani also demonstrate, the body will not be so easily disposed of. If we pull the plug on gender, if we drain race of any meaning, we are still left with the material facts and fictions of the body—with the different ifs, ands, and butts of different bodies. It is easy enough to theorize difference in the abstract, to posit "the body" in one discourse or another. But in the face of real bodies, ease quickly expands into complexity. To put the question in disquietingly personal terms: From the ivory towers of the academy I can criticize the racist fictions inscribed in Shani's false bottom from now until retirement, but shopping for jeans in Filene's Basement, how am I to escape the physical fact of my own steatopygic hips? Do the facts of my own body leave me hoisted, not on my own petard, perhaps, but on my own haunches?

We need to theorize race and gender not as meaning*less* but as meaning*ful*—as sites of difference, filled with constructed meanings that are in need of constant decoding and interrogation. Such analysis may not finally free us of the ubiquitous body-biology bind or release us from the quagmire of racism and sexism, but it may be at once the most and the least we can do to reclaim difference from the molds of mass production and the casts of dominant culture.

Yet, if the process of deconstruction also constructs, tearing Barbie down runs the risk of building Barbie up—or reifying difference in much the same way that commodity culture does. Rather than representing a critical kiss of death, readings that treat Barbie as a real threat to womankind—a harbinger of eating and shopping disorders—actually breathe life into the doll's plastic form. This is not to say that Barbie can simply be reduced to a piece of plastic. It is to say that hazard lies less in buying Barbie than in buying into Barbie, internalizing the larger mythologies of gender and race that make possible both the "like me" of Barbie and its critique. So, if this is a cautionary tale, the final watchword for consumers and critics alike must be not only *caveat emptor* but also *caveat lector:* Let the buyer and the reader beware.

$\mathcal{W}$hat on earth is Barbie doing in synagogue? Well, she is a Jewish girl, after all, created by a Jewish couple and named for another Jewish girl, Mattel cofounder Ruth Handler's daughter, Barbara. Still, her appearance in synagogue on Yom Kippur, the most holy and sober of the Jewish holidays, seems more than a little strange.

But in this essay, Rabbi Susan Schnur draws from her own experience in the pulpit to explain how and why Barbie came to her synagogue one particular Yom Kippur. Although Barbie was not an anticipated congregant, her arrival allowed for some unexpected insights about the meaning of the day, and ultimately about the imperfect, tattered fabric of our spiritual lives.

BARBIE DOES YOM KIPPUR

Rabbi Susan Schnur

Some years ago, when I was fresh out of seminary and installed in my first pulpit, I nourished a number of stupid ideas about synagogue life—not the least of which was the idea that kids should do whatever they want during religious services. That's right, *whatever they want*. I based this ridiculous notion on my own childhood congregational experience—years and years of weekly shul-going, during which time I never so much as *once* cracked open a prayerbook. What I did do, however, *religiously*—what a whole loose-knit bunch of us kids did every Sabbath at synagogue, *religiously*, was smash each other with the sanctuary's swinging doors, hold shrieking matches in the stairwells, toss all the fur coats in the cloakroom into one huge pile and bury ourselves, crawl under and over bathroom stalls in strict monastic sequences, terrify each other in the industrial kitchen's enormous walk-in freezer, and play checkers on the parquet floor of the elegant shul vestibule with *yahrtzeit* glasses purloined from the custodial closet.

Years after these anarchic Sabbaths, when, as a grown-up, I

would occasionally bump into an old shul-crony, we would immediately rush into blabbing contentedly about those long-ago long-shadowed tumbleweed Saturdays—orthodox, of course, in their own scrupulous fashion—and we'd marvel about how our luxurious *Shabbos* antics had translated for us, for all of us—effortlessly, cozily—into a bedrock love of religion.

Thus it was with complete confidence that I headed into my first Yom Kippur as a full-fledged rabbi, inviting children to bring whatever they wanted to the season's long penitential services: Barbies, Lotto, He-Men, comic books, *Pat the Bunny.* That year's haunting Kol Nidre service, I remember, felt particularly spiritual and introspective: lights low, Torahs held aloft by ancient *zeidehs* (grandpas) whose davvening (praying) was mood-alteringly Yiddish-inflected, the feel in the sanctuary lean, the medieval chant spellbinding, almost primevally genetic . . . when *kaboom!!!,* an ear-splitting volley of machine-gun fire hit the room, and I wheeled around to see my own rotten child, age four, gunning down all the Jews in the sanctuary with his man-sized Toys "R" Us weapon. My husband yanked the kid out the door, and the room became abruptly, tensely silent. There *is* historic precedent, after all, for Jews being shot, burned, beaten, raped, starved, frozen, et cetera, in locked Ashkenazy shuls during the Days of Awe. Why wasn't this kid playing red-light, green-light in his fuzzy-wuzzy socks on the wall-to-wall Berber like a *good* little recreant? What happened to checkers?

But heavy-duty weaponry, it turned out, was not the only arsenal being built up that Yom Kippur. While the boys stockpiled their counterphobic fantasy objects—that is, those items of play that children gravitate toward in order to master their anxieties about someday being full grown-ups who run the world, who win—the girls were amassing theirs, in the form of Barbies, those beautiful women with "female power" who the girls hoped one day to become. By the next morning at shul, there were dozens of Barbies in attendance; leggy Trojan horses in the High Holiday wings, they were virginal, masochistic, eager to offer themselves sacrificially on the Yom Kippur altar.

Barbie's formal religious debut, however, did not occur until the near-end of the holy day, at twilight—at which dust-motey hour the sanctuary is no longer a roomful of individuals praying but rather a single fossil organism that breathes, a palliation of survivors, a lump of gatekeepers against the silence of the universe, glazed guardians of the human promise to *be* in this world. Those of us who had lasted twenty-five hours had stood, sat, bowed, chanted, ritually beaten our breasts with our fists, and intoned hour after endless hour—tired, thirsty, very bored, hungry, irritable, malodorous—until finally dusk began to hint at our reward: Catharsis, Renewal, Virtue, Serenity, Purity, Love.

Suddenly, though, as we lugubriously cranked out the final "Our Father, our King, we have sinned before Thee," dragging the syllables so that our crowning prayer would coincide with the achingly slow filibuster of the dying sun, we heard a stampeding racket above our heads, painfully reminiscent of the awfulness of the previous night's shrill gunfire. Wasting not a second, I ran out the door, up the Hebrew-school steps, and there, in flagrante delicto, I caught sight of dozens of girls, little girls, very little girls—the oldest, maybe eleven—barreling up and down the hall holding Barbies. They were racing, up and back, up and back, clutching Barbies.

"Let me guess," I said to the girls breathlessly, hushing them and gathering them around. "Barbie's exercising." They nodded. "Why?" I continued rhetorically, still panting. "Because, let me guess, she fasted for Yom Kippur." They nodded again.

"Barbie is exercising off some last-minute pounds before she breaks the fast by bingeing on all the food they're setting up downstairs. You smell it?" They nodded. "Am I right?" "Yeah." *Our rabbi knows everything!* I imagined them thinking. I considered, in my own head, the nature of epiphany. Was my discernment of the meaning of the girls' play a theosophical insight sent to me by the Lord God Himself, King of the Bathroom Scales, deeply male Ruler of the Universe, Who loves virgins and nonvirgins alike, so long as they all stand naked before Him, genuflecting to better read the little numbers, praying for the miracle of the lost half pound, surrendering themselves before His all-critical Power? This God, I thought problematically, *loves* complicitous girls who are preoccupied by self-loathing and utterly stupid tiny meaningless things. No, I think, my quick take on the meaning of Barbie's weight-reduction marathon was not a religious epiphany at all, but rather a reflexive lurch toward warped bulimic logic, derived from a combination, in this circumstance, of the previous night's gendered shoot-out and my own plummeting heart. Downstairs we were fasting for moral redemption, and upstairs we were fasting for Ken.

Suddenly, the girls started a spontaneous chant—Barbie's Kol Nidre, I guess—holding the dolls, modern iconic war goddesses, at flat chest-height, and militarily marching them down the hall: "I/Lost/the *Most*/Weight. I/Lost/the *Most*/Weight. . . ."

"Look," I said to them in summary, crouching to their level to impart a final piece of resigned rabbinic wisdom. "If you're going to run around, take off your shoes."

As I headed back down to the chapel in my white *kittel,* the special garment that is the color of mercy, worn only on the Day of Atonement, I heard a precocious five-year-old avouch nasally, "My Barbie *wins.*"

It was this kid—*this kid*—who I credit finally with ruining my entire spiritual year.

There are many ways to understand the role Barbie played that Day of Atonement, but what struck me then was that *my* childhood synagogue impieties felt worlds apart from that of these kids'. *Our* actings-out had to do with the absolute safety and all-encompassing coherence of our religious, liberal, white, middle-class, American, 1950s lives—exemplified by the Sabbath but present *every* day. On *Shabbos,* parking our parents (and their parents, and virtually every grown-up we knew) with God as babysitter, we had the *preconditions* for running amok, for our unruly intoxications at the margins. Our palimpsest was *simpler* than met the eye; Barbie's, though, is more complicated.

Barbie, Toys "Я" Us machine guns—these are "charged objects," contaminative; they represent the dog-eat-dog world, the obsessively competitive culture that synagogues and mosques and churches strive to keep *out*. Barbie expresses the dilemmas of our desires, the sustained dissonance in our lives between the spiritual and the materialistic, the emotional gridlock inherent in our culture of relentless individualism. Barbie is a concretization of what the critic Walter Lippmann called, as far back as 1929, "the acids of modernity"; she strands us in narcissism, self-esteem struggles, the empty victories of consumerism. The kiddy-instigated pollutions at my latter-day shul (not my childhood one) involved gendered mastery exercises around the dialectical themes of domination/control, violence/beauty, sexuality/power, love/envy, aggression toward the self and toward the other.

In my childhood shul, our developmental task felt quite different: We kids used the synagogue the way babies use parents' laps: to be rocked, soothed, reassured, to be filled up with love and emotional security, to be steeped in the predictable *because* it is developmentally empowering.

Then again, these interpretations are all, perhaps, beside the point. I could as easily say that the theme of Yom Kippur *is* "the acids of modernity," *is* contamination, since the liturgy is all about the construction of contrasts: pure vs. impure, obedience vs. rebellion, order vs. disorder, Life vs. Death. To quote the seminal High Holiday prayer,

> On Rosh Hashana the decree is inscribed and on Yom Kippur it is sealed, who shall live and who shall die, who shall perish by fire and who by water, who by sword and who by beast, who by hunger and who by thirst, who shall have rest and who shall go wandering, who shall be tranquil and who shall be disturbed. . . .

The penitential season is one of purification, a realigning of everything that is out of whack, a killing off of what's "bad." This is why the Israelite priests took the famous ur-scapegoat and drove it into the wilderness with all the people's sins on its head, to chase out all that was impure, to cleanse. The word *kippur* itself means "purge"—to purge ourselves of anxieties and dissatisfactions, to choose a new course in life, to purify. Maybe even binge and purge—one of Barbie's specialties.

Perhaps the girls running laps with their Barbies at synagogue, exercising addictively, fasting, were pointing out the hypocrisies of religious life—that our penance doesn't really change us, that our "fasts" are feel-good catharses that fail to generalize into our real lives, that fasts only set up binges, penitence only sets up the next reactive round of guilty indulgences.

It could be that we need *more* Barbies and war toys at our religious services in order to mock our prayers, to shove into our faces the entrenched hear-no-evil/see-no-evil ethos that religious life secretly sanctions. As we read (on Yom Kippur) from the prophet Isaiah, "Is such the fast I desire, a day for people to starve their bodies? No. *This* is the fast I desire: to loose the fetters of injustice." Or maybe, if I had been speedier of mind at Barbie's anorectic Yom Kippur debut, I could have gathered up all the dolls and all the plastic weapons, put all our community's sins upon them, and driven them into the wilderness with great ceremony, or burned them, or thrown them off a cliff, or put them in the recycling bin and thought about that. How to restore Eden. Next year in Jerusalem. All that stuff.

As I sit at my desk finishing up this essay, my son, now tall and sixteen, reads over my shoulder. "I think you have it wrong, Ma," he concludes. "You know that Chassidic story about the illiterate shepherd boy who comes to synagogue on Yom Kippur but he doesn't know how to pray? Finally, he just takes out his shepherd's flute in synagogue and blows it as hard as he can, and the people freak out because it's forbidden to play instruments on the most holy day of the year. But the rabbi says, 'This boy's prayer, more than ours, will *certainly* reach Heaven, because he prays from the gut.'

"I remember that incident in shul when I was four," he continues, "and Dad came from nowhere and yanked me out to the parking lot. Maybe I was praying with that machine gun. Maybe we pray with our violence; we pray with our anorexia. We pray." He shrugs.

"That's lovely," I say to my wonderful son who once gunned down a roomful of worshipers. And I put it in my essay.

POSTMODERN MUSE

With the rise of status from mere doll to cultural icon, Barbie has become a postmodern muse onto which visual artists, fiction writers, and, not least of all, poets have projected their imaginative voices. Poets Jeanne Marie Beaumont and David Trinidad, whose work appears here, have both been collectors of vintage Barbies. Denise Duhamel's poems represent only three of the forty-three she has written and which appear in Kinky, *a volume of poetry whose exclusive subject is Barbie.*

PHOTOGRAPHING THE DOLLS

Jeanne Marie Beaumont

I wanted to invent a record,
one worth filing in a historical museum
of the future age.
If there was light from the window,
I used that,
or if lamps were lit
lending golden tints of posterity, good, good.

I pursued true illusion—
a recreation where the fake
takes on the psychic heft of the past.
Through each nuance of position: head
tilt, glance sideways,
balance on a half-inch foot
          —Look, I realize
they might all seem the same to you,
but I was schooled in subtle-
ties, out of fashion at the time as Latin

or home ec, which I skipped.
If you fail
          to be charmed, it
matters little.
For myself I shod them, posed them,
shot them, exposed them.
From me they received books to read,
bouquets, a made bed, dessert.
I hung their walls with paper and pictures
and built them a room. Gave them friends
in abundance, conversations freeze-
framed for their tiny eternity.

Soon, a house. That is, many rooms.
The house made these words.

OF MERE PLASTIC

David Trinidad

for Wayne Koestenbaum

The Barbie at the end of the mind,
Beyond the last collectible, is dressed
In "Golden Glory" (1965–1966),

A gold floral lamé empire-styled
Evening dress with attached
Green chiffon scarf and

Matching coat with fur-trimmed
Neckline and sequin/bead
Detail at each side. Her accessories:

Short white gloves, clear shoes
With gold glitter, and a hard-to-find
Green silk clutch with gold filigree

Braid around the center of the bag.
It closes with a single golden button.
The boy holds her in his palm

And strokes her blonde hair.
She stares back without feeling,
Forever forbidden, an object

Of eternal mystery and insatiable
Desire. He knows then
That she is the reason

That we are happy or unhappy.
He pulls the string at the back
Of her neck; she says things like

"I have a date tonight!"
And "Let's have a fashion show
Together." Her wardrobe case

Overflows with the fanciest outfits:
"Sophisticated Lady," "Magnificence,"
    "Midnight Blue."
3 hair colors. Bendable legs too!

The doll is propelled through outer space,
A kind of miniature Barbarella.
She sports "Miss Astronaut" (1965),

A metallic silver fabric suit
(The brown plastic straps at the shoulders
And across the bodice feature

Golden buckles) and two-part
White plastic helmet. Her accessories:
Brown plastic mittens,

Zip boots, and sheer nylon
Mattel flag, which she triumphantly sticks
Into another conquered planet.

PLANNING THE FANTASY WEDDING

Denise Duhamel

"You're the only one for me," Barbie says, trying to bend
her arms enough to hug Ken. They're getting married
in only a month, and Barbie's confident she's made
the right choice. Because she's blond, she chose the dark
haired male fashion doll as her husband-to-be. Skipper
wants silk roses in her flower-girl bouquet, so Barbie
has to remember to call the florist to change her order.
The photographer is paid in installments, which is
    considerate,
but Barbie has to mark in her day book when to send in
   the checks.
She doesn't want Ken to throw her garter,
sure he will degrade all the women at the reception
in the process, but try to tell that to the deejay
who thinks the gesture is funny and cute. He insists
if Ken doesn't throw the garter, the guests will feel
   ripped off.
The bridesmaids' gowns finally fit the bridesmaids,

but now their shoes have to be dyed—and Barbie
has chosen a hard fantasy color, watermelon, that
      sometimes comes out
too light or too dark. The baker won't put the fresh
      flowers
on the cake unless they're arranged on a ring, so Barbie
      has to call the florist
again. Should the pew bows go on every other row?
Will they be too gaudy if there are too many?
Will Barbie and Ken look cheap if they skip? The
      premarital
counseling is next week, with the minister
who will ask them questions, trying to find their
      fundamental
differences, and remind them that married life is not
always a bed of roses. Barbie's gown has to be altered,
at the hem and the sleeves. It's at least three trips—
an initial fitting, a basting, then full stitches. The
      seamstress
has already had to cancel once because of problems with
      her ex-husband
which leaves a funny feeling in Barbie's stomach.
Barbie and Ken finally find traditional matching rings,
that aren't etched or brushed with a 90s mall look.
She makes her nail appointment for the day before the
      wedding
and the manicurist reminds her to be careful of her
      hands
between now and then. She has to get up at six
the day of the ceremony to have her hair curled into a
      bun and to starch
her veil so it poufs out enough. She had to hire
a second pianist because the first one didn't know all the
      music.
She has to call the honeymoon hotels and reserve rooms
with her Visa. She has to pick up the airline tickets

and find a good restaurant for the rehearsal dinner.
She and Ken had to look through the minister's prayer
    books
deciding the format of the mass. They weren't sure
whether to have communion, who of their guests would
    partake.
The replies come back so slowly, Barbie complains.
Her friends on the phone say they'll be there, but never
send their RSVPs. The friends who write they are
    coming
call back later to cancel with all kinds of excuses. Some
    want to let her know
at the last minute. Others say it depends on the price of
    airfare
or the health of their babies or cats. At breakfast,
Barbie finds herself snippy because of something
small that Ken says. As she times her hard boiled egg,
the pressure mounts. She cries out her wish—that all
    she had left to do was to look good in a rented tux.

HOLOCAUST BARBIE

Denise Duhamel

Barbie was born after World War II,
in the midst of its consequences—disgruntled women
back in their United States' kitchens. Barbie'd
only heard of the overseas atrocities, but was more
    certain
she was reincarnated with each horror story, with each
    little pang
of her déjà-vu. Her Aryan air, the ease in
which her arm, unable to bend at the elbow,
would salute. The terror when she saw a pile
of dolls like herself, naked and dirty, in the mass grave of
    a toy chest.
Barbie sought hypnotists and healers,
who all saw the connection, though none could be sure
whether in her past Barbie was the Nazi or the Jew.

BARBIE'S GYN APPOINTMENT

Denise Duhamel

Her high arches defy the stirrups
and her legs refuse to open wide.
She has no complaints, cramps,
spottings, or flashes. It doesn't hurt
when the doctor presses on her abdomen.
There's nowhere for him to take a Pap smear,
but Barbie's gynecologist suggests a D and C,
a hysterectomy, then a biopsy, just to be sure.
Barbie rebels as her breasts refuse to give
under the weight of the mammogram machine's plate.
She doesn't own a nightie suitable
for hospital wear, she explains, as she refuses operations
and scrunches the disposable examining frock
into a ball. She tosses it into the trash can
with relief. Not even Barbie looks good
in that pale green. She'll skip her follow-up appointment
on behalf of the rest of us who can't

and circle the globe, a tiny copy of *The New Our Bodies,*
Ourselves under her arm. The book will fire her
    imagination,
each chapter a fashion doll's version of the best science
    fiction.

After you've said everything there is to say about Barbie's body, there is still the subject of her marvelous, inventive, and constantly changing clothes. In the 1950s, they showed echoes of Dior and Balenciaga; by the late 1990s, they owe more to Madonna and the Spice Girls.

Melissa Hook muses on the meanings of Barbie's clothes, both for her and the other women in her family, particularly her frosty but fashion-conscious grandmother.

MATERIAL GIRL

Melissa Hook

As a little girl, the only clue I had that my grandmother knew I existed was the fact that she gave me beautiful dolls. During my family's biannual visits to her home, our conversations were limited to yes-pleases and no-thank-yous; there were no affectionate hugs or cuddles, and the only kisses she gave me were obligatory lip-to-lip pecks from which I twisted with discomfort. She was a sharp-tongued and stern second-generation German matriarch who ran her family with an iron hand, eliciting absolute fealty from her children and terrifying her grandchildren. When I was five, however, she began to charm me with dolls, and although her early efforts to form an emotional bond with me missed the mark, when she introduced Barbie, and more specifically Barbie's wardrobe, into my life, our relationship blossomed.

In those days, I had a reputation for ritually destroying with pen and ink body tattoos and excessive hair brushing every rubber baby that came my way. My mother had banned new doll purchases on my behalf, yet to my surprise, each time I arrived in Texas for the summer visit, I found a perfect, pristine Madame Alexander laid out on the spare bed in my room, along with a wardrobe of lovely handmade doll fashions: fancy dresses, pearl-buttoned underwear, lace-trimmed negligees, and silk-brocade evening wear. Having purchased the doll months in advance, Grandmother had spent winter evenings creating stylish miniature garments for her from leftover dress fabrics. The Alexanders were hard to relate to—they were expensive toys, meant to be admired and enjoyed in a ladylike manner—and although I could change their outfits, the clothes (like the dolls), reminded me of Mamie Eisenhower. When I liked a doll, I could become her in an imaginary sense, and I preferred to be a glamorous Rita Hayworth or a winsome Sleeping Beauty.

While projecting onto Madame Alexander dolls was limited because I found them stodgy and old-fashioned, they nevertheless provided me with entertainment during the searing hot July afternoons when the rest of my family was napping. No doubt, from Grandmother's point of view, the doll play improved my loutish, tomboy nature. The Alex dolls never stripteased; they dressed for tea; they never cussed or shouted; they were gracious and soft-spoken. They provided me with an opportunity to act out the type of genteel behavior that Grandmother clearly encouraged.

In those days, invitations to the young-lady luncheons, swim parties, and movie dates that Grandmother's friends arranged as entertainment for the visiting granddaughters required that I improve my awkward behavior. Growing up in my "Yankee" family, I had become argumentative and confrontational as soon as I could speak. And it was obvious among the gentility of Paris, Texas, that negative comments and jokes at the expense of others were inappropriate. As soon as I learned to suppress sarcasm and to skillfully flatter, however, the invitations flowed. I would say "You look especially nice today, Mrs. Dees," when she actually looked terrible. Or I might have gushed about a playmate's dopey new toy, not because I liked it but because I knew she would enjoy the compliment. I gave up shorts and T-shirts for frilly dresses, cultured pearls, and white gloves, and if you ignored my frizzy hair and angel-wing eyeglasses, I looked like a Madame Alexander doll when I went out to parties.

The arrival of Barbie, however, provoked a dramatic change in Grandmother's focus. No sooner had she discovered the brunette babe than she abandoned the Alexanders. It is doubtful, however, that she meant to modify my behavior with Mattel's new version of a sexy German comic-strip porn star. I was too immature in 1960, when the first Barbie arrived by post (wearing a skintight black torch-singer gown, spiked heels, and pink scarf dangling off her bare shoulders), to know that she was sexy. My prim and proper grandmother was charmingly oblivious to the doll's blatant sexuality, choosing to overlook what the large breasts, narrow waist, and tiny round buttocks conveyed for the pleasure taken in the doll's glamorous wardrobe. She surprised me with not one but two Barbies in the first year, and demonstrating an extravagance inconsistent with her frugal nature, bought every outfit in the first catalog.

Lust for clothes is a contagious disease. Once my mother moved away from Paris and started a family, she became an incorrigible sale shopper who managed to wear designer clothes purchased with the dollars skimmed from her young married's food budget. As for me, as soon as I discovered, in a cardboard box in the attic, Mother's old sorority-girl crêpe-de-chine evening dresses in shades of apricot, marigold, and avocado green, I was hooked on glamour. Like Barbie's black-sequined gown, each dress was packed with a matching evening wrap and a pair of elbow-length gloves. Their delicately beaded bodices and slim-fitting, bias-cut skirts pinned tightly around my sticklike body triggered a clothes meme in my DNA and I became Greta Garbo. With the appearance of raven-haired Barbie in her dramatic dress, I found an alter ego who wore fabulous clothes, and any chance I had of growing up immune to the lust for the perfect cut disappeared forever.

In my family, receiving gifts meant writing thank-you notes, and during the initial rush to collect Barbie outfits, I wrote letters to Grandmother on a monthly basis. By age nine, I knew that an acceptable thank-you note required either creative or emotional content. "You are the best grandmother in the world, I love you," worked only once, so I chatted about Barbie clothes to make the letters more interesting: "How much I appreciated the detail of the striped red lining of the linen jacket of the 'Busy Gal' outfit" and "Wouldn't it be wonderful if I could wear her matching orange virgin wool sweater set with my gray flannel wraparound." Her letter in reply might have mentioned the tailoring of the airline-stewardess jacket that she had given to me for my birthday. By the end of the second month, something like Enchanted Evening would have arrived in the mail, and I would be gearing up for another scintillating thank-you.

Grandmother and I embarked upon a rich, satisfying relationship sustained by our enthusiasm for doll fashion. As I became a devoted granddaughter, she revealed the affectionate nature and gentle sense of humor behind her austere facade. Hugs and squeezes accompanied her once-detestable kisses. If we discussed Barbie outfits, I could engage her attention: She would look at my face and take my comments seriously. And when I ripped the doll clothing, instead of reprimanding me, she would tease me about the poor Barbie from across the tracks and then teach me how to make the tiny hand stitches required to repair the torn items. Her influence over my doll play was such that while my girlfriends were arranging sex dates for Barbie and Ken in Kleenex-box cars in their closets, I was dreaming about how lovely I'd look in the pink satin evening gown or the blue corduroy jumper. Ken was something of a loser, in my mind, and sex was not a word in my vocabulary.

Looking back, I shouldn't be the least bit surprised as the desire for great clothes has frequently reached the level of addiction among the women in my family, including Grandmother. By the time I got to know her, she had become a closet clothes horse, appearing daily in her sturdy black pumps and calf-length shirtwaist dresses, never baring a knee or exposing a shoulder. But I had found her gorgeous, silver-beaded and sequined flapper dress preserved in tissue paper in the guest-room cupboard, and even though the bosom-exposing side slits had been filled in with silver lamé fabric, Grandmother certainly had shown a lot of thigh when she wore that dress. Donning it to dance the Charleston, she must have been downright daring. Even photographs of her 1912 wedding show a gown more elaborate than Princess Diana's.

Married life in rural Texas soon limited her opportunities to wear glamorous garments, and as a mature woman and excellent seamstress, she satisfied her addiction when she purchased lush fabrics and transformed them into stylish suits, dresses, and lovely evening wear for her two daughters. They dressed like Hollywood starlets in the 1940s. By then, however, the pursuit of glamour was a means to an end—an engaging group activity that entertained her daughters while it enhanced her bond with them as kindred females. Back-bedroom fashion shows and home beauty sessions were regular weekend events where the sharing of beauty tips and the exchange of advice developed a wonderful intimacy among them.

Today, I am still something of a Barbie enthusiast. Although I don't play with the dolls in my collection—I preserve them for their sentimental value—I do inspect and marvel at the original, well-designed wardrobe and the quality of its fabrication. The clothes lust they triggered in my brain has never subsided, and like my mother, I am an avid sale shopper. With the exception of an occasional in-season splurge, I am a dedicated Barney's warehouse–sale fan, and have been known to plan my trips to visit friends in Texas to coincide with the Last Call sale at Neiman Marcus in Dallas.

The Madame Alexanders live in a Chinese armoire in the foyer. Grandmother's porcelain-headed infant from the 1890s has a spot on a shelf, and her 1920s Italian felt doll with the hand-painted eyes watches over me from a corner chair in the living room. It was doll play rather than doll collecting, however, that established my friendship with Grandmother. We replicated the warm, cozy feeling of a back-bedroom fashion show improvising with a couple of big-bosomed Barbies and a Mattel box full of fabulous outfits. Nurse Barbie, Stewardess Barbie, Nightclubber Barbie, and Bridal Barbie, plus the spectacular Barbies we imagined, all had a part to play in a crazy little world we divined so that my grandmother, the epitome of Texas gentility, and I could play the glamour game. And together we celebrated the ritual cultivation of beauty that has created closeness among women since time immemorial.

Barbie is most emphatically a fully grown woman doll, as opposed to the baby and toddler dolls that tend to dominate—at least in sheer numbers—the market. The meaning of this baby doll/woman doll split, and its ramifications for little girls, is analyzed by scholar Sherrie A. Inness in "Barbie Gets a Bum Rap: Barbie's Place in the World of Dolls."

BARBIE GETS A BUM RAP: BARBIE'S PLACE IN THE WORLD OF DOLLS

Sherrie A. Inness

You see her everywhere. Books are devoted to her. She appears in commercials. There are college courses that focus entirely on her history. She even has a complete aisle in Toys "R" Us solely for her and her booty. Barbie is omnipresent. Without a doubt, she is the most discussed and debated doll in the world. This overwhelming interest in Barbie, however, obscures the fact that she is only one of many dolls in any local toy store. To understand Barbie and the messages she conveys to girls, you need to venture beyond the Barbie aisle in the toy store, into the adjoining aisles where a horde of other dolls are jammed into the shelves. No matter whether you love or hate Barbie, the only way to understand her place in the world is to examine how she fits into the much larger world of dolls.

This world of dolls has been little examined by scholars.[1] The most important study about girls and dolls is Miriam Formanek-Brunell's *Made to Play House: Dolls and the Commercialization of American Girlhood, 1830–1930* (1993), one of many important works to come out in the booming field of girls' studies.[2] It is unfortunate that little research has been accomplished, because the societal importance of dolls (and toys in general) is underestimated, and dolls "continue to be typically misunderstood as trivial artifacts of a commercialized girls' culture."[3] Other than *Made to Play House*, the research on dolls is skimpy, and the majority of the work has been done on Barbie—the doll scholars love to bash. They scoff at her ludicrous body proportions and roll their eyes at her Day-Glo pink outfits and her itsy-bitsy high heels on which she seems always to be tottering. With her bleached-blond hair and her dream-girl figure, Barbie seems to have not a care in the world other than whether she should go to the beach or the mall for the afternoon. Barbie seems hardly like a desirable model for a young girl to emulate, and some of my friends will go to any length to get Barbie and her empire of pink paraphernalia out of their homes. But is Barbie all bad? Is she as terrible a role model as we sometimes assume?

Strolling through Toys "Я" Us one day, I began to recognize that Barbie, particularly when seen in the context of other dolls, was not as evil as I had assumed. Much to my amazement, I began to recognize that the doll so many people love to hate might convey some surprisingly positive messages to young girls, messages that might be far more empowering and enabling than those conveyed by many other dolls. Even more surprising, I discovered that Barbie was actually a more realistic role model than other dolls. Barbie? Realistic?! I hear some people gasp in disbelief, but Barbie is realistic in many ways, despite her unrealistic proportions. She does, after all, hold jobs, drive cars, garden, take vacations, own homes, and perform many other chores adults need to accomplish. And her jobs aren't only traditional female ones such as being a nurse or a stewardess. Now a young girl may go "looking for dinosaurs with Paleontologist Barbie." In her perky khaki shorts with matching hat and her coordinating pink scarf and pink canteen, Barbie isn't exactly as rough-and-tumble as Indiana Jones, but at least her work is less stereotypical than teaching first-graders. The same Career Collection also includes Pilot Barbie and Dentist Barbie. If these careers seem too tame, NASCAR Barbie (introduced in 1998) has a career as a race-car driver. Barbie allows young girls to explore a number of careers and, more important, suggests that such careers are perfectly acceptable for girls and women.

And it's a good thing that Barbie is employed, because she needs a lucrative job to pay for her garage packed with vehicles, including a Hot Drivin' Sports Car, Fun for 4 Car, Porsche Boxster, Cruisin' Car, and Hot Stylin' Motorcycle. Barbie's buying spree doesn't end there. She is also a travel junkie who seems to go on a vacation every week. She travels to an exotic resort where she spends time in her bubbling spa. Hula Hair Barbie, with her hula skirt and her barely there bikini top, is obviously not working a nine-to-five job. Barbie's packed garage and her jet-set adventures are often pointed out as examples of her incredible consumption habits. People argue that Barbie teaches girls that purchasing commodities is the only way to be successful and have fun, but Barbie's consumption also teaches other lessons. Barbie is about movement and action. She tells girls that it is fun and exciting for them to have adventures, even hopping on their Hot Stylin' Motorcycles and heading for the open road.

Only when I began to wander down the other aisles of the local toy store did I fully recognize that Barbie's messages about the importance of action and adventure were far superior to the messages conveyed by other dolls. The biggest difference between Barbie's aisle and the others can be summed up in one word: *babies.* In the other aisles, baby dolls were everywhere; in Barbie's aisle, babies were almost nonexistent. Paleontologist Barbie or Pilot Barbie would be hard pressed to drag along a baby to the workplace. Even when Barbie is getting dressed for a night on the town with Ken, she obviously doesn't want to lug a baby along. This nearly baby-free existence is a world away from what you discover in other aisles, where it is impossible to escape babies, even for a minute. On one side, I was confronted by the popular Cabbage Patch Kids—all babies. On the other side, a wall full of Dream Garden dolls loomed over me. Again, all the Dream Garden dolls were babies, including Strawberry Sweetie, Peach Sweetie, Caramel Apple Sweetie, and Blueberry Sweetie. I was getting a sugar overdose, so I needed to move on. But I didn't escape the babies: Magic Stroller Baby, Make Me Better Baby, Coochy Coo Baby and Stroller, Baby Pick Me Up, Bedtime Bottle Baby, Baby So Beautiful, and many others. I was surrounded by baby dolls that all conveyed the same message: having a baby is the greatest experience of a woman's life, and every girl should want a baby more than anything else. These dolls didn't teach about the importance of travel and adventure; they taught about the importance of maternity and domesticity. They also conveyed the completely unrealistic message that babies are all a woman (or a girl) needs for complete bliss. Lessons like this can lead many girls to have babies while still teenagers, thinking that children are enough to fill someone's life with joy. Only when it is sometimes too late do many young mothers realize that perhaps they wanted some of the adventure and excitement that Barbie and her pals enjoy.

I moved down the aisle. Perhaps the Sky Dancers, another popular group of dolls, would have a bit more going on in their lives than the baby dolls who spent their lives cooing, giggling, crying, and uttering their first words. The Sky Dancers could "really dance and fly in the air," as one package claimed. They also performed other small feats. Sky Dancer Eleni's ribbons swirl around her as she flies. Sky Dancer Sunbeam lights up as she flies. Sky Dancer Moon Shimmer flies through the air after being launched like a rocket. These gals—no surprise—do not live in Barbie's house or her Malibu condo. They spend most of their time flying through the air. They wouldn't be a good mortgage risk, unlike Barbie with her plethora of jobs. The Sky Dancers teach lessons about the importance of being beautiful, elegant, graceful, and feminine; they teach very little about the possibilities that girls can grow up to be dentists and pilots and buy condos and cars. Who would you rather have your girl mimic?

Of course, you might still assume that dolls and other toys simply don't matter. A girl can play with any doll she wants, and it will not make a difference to her when she's older. But toys do matter, and they do convey ideas about how adult life should be run. As French cultural theorist Roland Barthes writes, "French toys always mean something, and this something is always entirely socialized, constituted by the myths or the techniques of modern adult life." He continues, "The fact that French toys literally prefigure the world of adult functions obviously cannot but prepare the child to accept them all, by constituting for him, even before he can think about it, the alibi of a Nature which has at all times created soldiers, postmen and Vespas."[4] Whether French or American, toys convey a great deal about how adults wish children to grow up, and, as Barthes observes, toys prepare us for the roles we wish children to think of as "natural." What roles do we wish girls to grow up and assume are "natural"? I want girls to challenge the notion that being mothers is the "natural" role open to them. I want girls to drive across the country in their sports cars; I want girls to travel around the world in planes they pilot themselves; I want girls to tackle difficult careers, like paleontology, that require grit, determination, and fierce intelligence. In other words, I want girls to be like Barbie.

OUR DAUGHTERS, THEIR BARBIES

*N*ot everyone played with Barbie. Some women were too old when she made her debut; others just weren't interested. But even women who didn't actually play with her had their own relationships with her, relationships that began when Barbie was placed in the hands of their daughters.

Written from the vantage point of initmate observer, these essays offer differing views of Barbie-play. Novelist Carol Shields is both tolerant and acerbic in her essay "I Believe in Dolls." In "You Can Never Have Too Many," novelist Jane Smiley maintains that Barbie taught her daughters things she couldn't even begin to imagine, while short-story writer Mariflo Stephens turned cartwheels of joy when she could say—and write—"Barbie Doesn't Live Here Anymore." Molly Jong-Fast, daughter of writer Erica Jong, remembers the "dysfunctional" Barbie she owned as a child in "Barbie: Twelve-Step Toy"; her mother's response, "Twelve Dancing Barbies," offers insights into the more magical meanings Barbie may have held for her child.

I Believe in Dolls

Carol Shields

I never actually played with Barbie dolls—already being an adult when they came on the market—but I feel almost certain I would have loved them in the same way my own daughters have loved them.

The love they bore them, though, was different from that pure, almost-human love they felt for their baby dolls. ("I believe in dolls," my four-year old daughter once confided to me, and I knew just what she meant: that she believed against all logic in their beating hearts and their ability to feel pain and accept comfort.)

Barbie dolls, on the other hand, were closer to being puppets, little mannequins to be moved about, dressed and undressed. My children, like children everywhere, played "house," that endless, formless, mythic game, in order to act out the drama of being grown-ups, and they used their Barbies as an answer, I think, to the fascination that all little girls have for the period that precedes adulthood, a teenage world that came blinking out of the television tube and through the words of popular songs.

Barbie dolls excited controversy from that first midcentury moment when they came on the market. We consumer-mothers were baffled by their instant success, since they lacked the sweetness, the vulnerability of traditional dolls. They were impossible to cuddle. But, it was said in Barbie's defense, she extended the period during which girls played with dolls. Formerly, girls had put away their dolls at age nine or ten; now twelve- and thirteen-year-olds were not embarrassed to be caught with their Barbies. This extension of childhood, or of innocent fantasy, was generally thought to be a "good thing."

Barbie dolls were condemned initially for being too fashion-oriented, but then it was remembered that paper dolls—and these had been around for a hundred years—were *all* about fashion and were completely uncuddleable as well. Probably no small child ever formed a bond with a paper doll.

The Barbies themselves were inexpensive, but their teensie-weensie clothes broke the bank. My mother-in-law came into action at this point, knitting entire miniature wardrobes, and I learned to look for bargain treasures at church bazaars where the making of Barbie clothes opened a whole new fund-raising window of opportunity. Where are all these tiny matched outfits today? Floating out there in space, in their own special Barbie-doll orbit.

The makers of Barbie dolls seemed, from the beginning, unconscionably opportunistic with their Barbie bedroom suites and Barbie space vehicles and the faked zeal and squeal of Barbie TV commercials, but these we managed to ignore in our household, opting only for the basic Barbie unit: pouting face, a bundle of stiffened hair, and a grotesque, unyielding body.

That body, of course, has been at the center of the Barbie wars, and with reason. Barbie-doll proportions, translated into human terms, offer up an appalling vision, and in that vision we can read something of the conflicting priorities of our society. Those breasts, that tiny waist, those long, slender, polished legs promise little girls a teenage future that is unreachable, at the same time toying with notions of sensuality that can only puzzle a little child.

But it is the face I've always found most eerily disturbing—with its dumb shine of self-absorption, its tripping tartish look of one who is out for all she can get. Barbie, icon of triviality, queen of consumer heaven. Dear old Barbie, the adolescent who never grew up.

You Can Never Have
Too Many

Jane Smiley

or my daughter's sixteenth birthday, my six-year-old son wanted to give her a Barbie. Barbies were on sale at the toy store for $9.99, and I gently guided him toward the Rapunzel Barbie, whose hair was so long that her head was cocked backward on her neck, or the Birthday Barbie, who had on a massive organdy skirt. The one he finally chose, way at the top, one I had not seen, was Baywatch Barbie. OK, she had a dolphin with her. I am willing to admit that that might have been the draw. But you know, Barbies are just all right with me. Maybe I have had more Barbies pass through my house than anyone. I like to think so. When A.J. wanted to bring another one home, I was glad, just for old times' sake. Lucy's Barbies went out with the trash two years ago, when we moved from Iowa to California, from girlhood to womanhood.

I was slightly too old for Barbie myself when they first came out in 1958—I was more of a stuffed animal girl, anyway—so my first real Barbie experience came when my twenty-year-old daughter was three. My First Barbie came home, and was disrobed. The clothes were lost. I spent the required amount of time deploring Barbie's proportions and coloring and the fact that her feet can only wear high heels. Barbie could not be shaped more differently from me, or have a more different weltanschauung from mine, but hey, *meni meni tekel upharsin,* here she came with all her stuff. The one I still remember most fondly was Twirly Curls Barbie. Like Rapunzel Barbie, Twirly Curls Barbie had a serious neck problem because of the weight of her hair. But she came with an intriguing pink-and-cream machine that attached to the ends of a couple of hanks of hair and twisted them together in a nice, though very large, chignon. The catch was that the hair had to be neatly combed for the machine to work, an impossible task for a four-year-old, so I spent a lot of time combing Barbie until I gave up. My daughters were not in the habit of shaving their Barbies' heads, but they could have. It's a good idea.

Both my girls went through periods where they would wear only pink and purple. I chalk this up to the Barbie influence. I preferred navy blue and red on them, myself. They also both learned to put on makeup before kindergarten. Lucy could lipstick her lips with her eyes closed and do it neatly, too, by the time she was five. I don't wear makeup. Nor do I have any gowns, bikinis, pink high heels, floral accessories, feminine furniture (like a dressing table or a pink chaise lounge). There are no blonds in my family. I never wear short shorts or feather boas or halter tops or off-the-shoulder peasant blouses. In other words, if my daughters were to learn certain Hollywood-inspired essentials of American womanhood, it wasn't going to be from me, it was going to be from Barbie. And so the Barbies came through the house in a flood. And I am here to tell you that Doctor Barbie was not one of them. Frilly, sexy, pink, purple, bedizened, and bejeweled were the preferred Barbies at my house, the more rhinestones the better. We had dozens of Barbies, because, frankly, Barbies are cheap in more ways than one.

My daughters had three mothers: me; their stepmother, who was not unlike me, stylistically; and Barbie. A friend of mine (male) maintains that Barbies have such staying power because they are the only anatomically adult dolls available, and children can manipulate and control them as they cannot the other adults in their lives. Yes. Perhaps for boys, toy soldiers offer the same pleasure. But I think girls like Barbies because through Barbie they can try on a no-holds-barred, all-stops-out model of femininity, and that is something they need to do, especially if their own mothers are more androgynous-looking and sober-dressing than Barbie can be. The more a girl is drawn to Barbie, the less, I think, she should be deprived of her, no matter what the child's mother's own values are. Longing is more likely to breed attachment than satisfaction is.

Finally, after some seventeen years, the Barbies in my house went the way of all flesh. In their last year with us, they were subject to any number of tragic narratives, at least partly inspired by that disguised Barbie literature, *Sweet Valley High.* One day, for example, I discovered the older girls showing the younger girls how to bandage the Barbies with toilet paper (gruesomely decorated with red nail polish) when they happened to get into alcohol-related car crashes with Ken. Barbie's sex life with Ken came under some scrutiny, as did Ken. But none of this was satisfactory. No doll in the toy box is less played with than Ken. That is because Barbie's relationships are only secondary to her sense of style, and little girls are far more interested in style far earlier.

My older daughter is twenty now. She wandered in the land of Barbie for many years—after all, Nancy Drew is a Barbie; Elizabeth and Jessica, the Sweet Valley Twins, are Barbies; Cinderella, Sleeping Beauty, Beauty of *Beauty and the Beast*, all are Barbies. The prettiest girl in school, always a blonde, or so it seems, is a Barbie, too. All the blondes on TV and in the movies are Barbies. A girl has to have Barbies in order to decide whether she herself wants to be a Barbie. On the one hand, she has the ever-present mom, who is wearing jeans, cutting her hair ever shorter, getting glasses at forty if not sooner, driving a dark-colored sedan, going to work or cleaning the house, or, worse, espousing all kinds of selfless values of hard work, charity, civic virtue, environmental responsibility. On the other hand, she has the ever-present Barbie, a tireless consumer whose favorite color is pink, whose jeans are much harder to get on her than her ballet tutu, whose hair requires constant care (always a pleasure for little girls who, to a woman, think they will surely go to beauty school), and who has more high heels than any First Lady of the Philippines who ever lived. Barbie represents, in every way, getting what you want when you want it, no matter who objects. Just after she stopped reading *Sweet Valley High* and passed her Barbies down to her younger sister, say, at about fourteen, my older daughter changed her views on her future. No longer did she plan to be a fashion consultant or a Hollywood movie star. No longer did beauty school attract her. She began to read authors like Sandra Cisneros and books like *Our Bodies, Ourselves,* by the Boston Women's Health Collective. She began her collection of all the works of U2, a band Barbie would *never* understand. She became socially conscious. She got to be the editor of her high school newspaper, not because it was a status position but because she had views she wanted to air on homophobia, the environment, and women's rights. Now she is planning to go to graduate school and law school and become an expert on women's health issues, perhaps adolescent health issues like anorexia and bulimia. She can go on for hours about women's problems with appearance and self-image. Barbie should be proud. My daughter wouldn't have gotten here without her.

Have we ever known a Barbie who, in the end, was cherished? I don't think so. More than all the other dolls in the toy box, perhaps because she isn't cuddly or sweet, Barbie is meant to be fiddled with, thought about, manipulated, done to. All of this aids in a girl's making up her mind about who she is and what she wants. That Barbie is a genius.

BARBIE DOESN'T LIVE
HERE ANYMORE

Mariflo Stephens

I've always known there was something wrong with Barbie. She looks nice enough. And she has her own Corvette, her own band, and her own dream house. Still, I just didn't want my daughter playing with her. But how can we snub Barbie? Little girls all over Charlottesville, all over Virginia, and, yes, all over the world, seem to be spending hour after hour with her.

I considered relying on my own experience. When, in 1962, I was presented with my first Barbie doll, I did what all the other little girls did with their Barbies: I took her clothes off. Wow! I could hardly wait to have a pair of my very own.

Then I put her clothes back on. It was hard. There was a snap the size of a pinhead and Barbie hardly cooperated. I pulled the tight dress up her legs, over her hips, and it stopped right there. Had a liquid Barbie been poured into this to harden? She was stiff as stone but still smelled like new rubber. I had to put her head between my teeth to get her dress past that chest. I was exhausted. But was it ever fun, I told myself.

Now where were those high heels and that pair of long white gloves? I found one glove. Later my friend Jane came over to play. She took the dress off, too. We waited for something to happen. Then we went out to climb some trees. Four hours later, we told our mothers we'd had a great time playing Barbie. (This was lobbying. Jane's mother looked quizzical and noted the leaves in our hair.)

I was twelve in 1962, so I didn't have too many good years left for Barbie. Soon I would *be* Barbie. I was blond, wasn't I? And I would be an American teenager with no time left for playing. My time would be devoted to the serious business of dressing and dating and talking on the telephone.

In the months to come, I made the best of it. I spent my entire piggybank savings on Barbie clothes—sequined evening gowns, fake-fur wraps, and high heels. The outfits had themes like Barbie Goes to the Prom and Barbie Steps Out printed in a fast-moving script with exclamation marks at the end. There wasn't much to do, however, but dress and undress Barbie, and I found I had to spend most of my time looking for a lost pink high heel the size of my little fingernail.

Buying the clothes was the exciting part. Since I liked horses, I picked out Barbie's rodeo skirt set with white high-heeled boots and fringe. These weren't Barbie's clothes, they were mine. If I could've worn Barbie's lavender loungewear with its pink feather boa to my seventh-grade classroom, I would have. If, that is, I could find it. Much was located under the sofa cushions, but far too late, I'm afraid.

Barbie retired early. I waited for my body to fill out, Barbie-style. My legs didn't grow to those proportions and neither did anything else. I got the idea that every time a teenage boy looked at me he saw only what was missing—what Barbie had that I didn't.

Even the blond hair didn't live up to expectations. Mine was fuzzy and its shape varied from day to day. Barbie's seemed to stay in a permanent coiffure. Evening gowns weren't even in style.

And not very many blondes can manage a nose that turns up that way.

Worst of all, Barbie doesn't do anything but lose her clothes.

I had wasted a lot of money, not to mention rich fantasy time, on a false goddess.

When my daughter, Jane, was born, I told myself there would be no false goddesses. I didn't name her after a goddess, I named her after the girl I'd climbed trees with.

When relatives started to inquire about birthday gifts, I didn't say "No Barbies, please," though I wanted to. I said instead that books were very nice gifts. I mentioned there wasn't much to do with a Barbie doll except comb her hair and I was sure we'd lose those little combs.

Jane turned seven. She had five Barbie dolls. I didn't see her playing with them much, although every few days I would find a pink high heel somewhere. I would spot the dolls around the house—their legs splayed crazily and scarves tied around their bodies for clothes.

One day Jane said: "Barbies don't do anything. They don't even bend their legs when you sit them down. Their legs stick straight out." I knew she was on to something. Then we cleaned up her room. I found most of the clothes and even some of the high heels. I was pretty proud of myself. But behind me I heard Jane saying: "Let's get rid of the Barbies."

"Huh?"

"They're dumb and prissy. They clutter up everything. Let's sell them."

"What do you mean by 'dumb and prissy'?"

"They look like this," she said and raised to tiptoe and smiled maniacally. "They've got globs of blue makeup over their eyes and they can't do anything. You can't even bend their legs to sit them on a model horse."

I seized the moment. "What else is wrong with the Barbies?"

"They don't have toes. Their shoes fall off. They're always on tiptoe."

"That would be tiring," I said, sympathetically.

"They never get tired. They don't do anything."

"What else is wrong?"

"They don't wear socks or pants. Just dresses or fish-net stockings or they go barefoot. All the commercials compliment their hair, but once their hair is tangled, it never goes back."

"Anything else wrong?" I asked—and here she won my heart if ever there was a contest for it.

"They're all the same age. There are no Barbie babies and no old people."

"Sounds like Barbie lives in a dull world," I said.

"No, not dull. Dumb and prissy. Let's sell them."

"How much should we charge for each one?"

"A penny," she said disgustedly, then immediately saw her error. "No, no. A dollar."

"Oh," I said, seeing my own error. Just because I considered Barbie small change didn't mean everyone else did. Six Barbies went out the back door to a secondhand shop and, in a matter of minutes, six dollars came in the front door.

Maybe Barbie's business suit with its one-inch briefcase inspired Jane's market wisdom.

After all, the new Barbies are still in stores, housed in pink boxes with bold script that seems to shout: Barbie Goes to the Office! My old dolls, with their narrow eyes and puckered lips, are upstairs like other mad women of the attic, whispering: "Who stole my feather boa?"

BARBIE, TWELVE-STEP TOY

Molly Jong-Fast

The first time anyone ever suspected there was something wrong with me was when they found my Barbie hanging upside down naked from my big yellow Tonka truck. I was four. I played with trucks. But most of the time I played with nothing at all.

Barbie was something other girls played with. Girls who ate dinner with their parents. Girls who had handsome older brothers, who played the game of Life with their families, and who had names like Cindy, Mindy, and Candy. I grew up in a town house filled with antiques. I grew up a Jew with a Chinese last name. I grew up in a silent house and most nights had dinner with a stoic nanny. Other people's Barbies were perfect; my Barbie was a little bit dysfunctional.

My Barbie grew up in boarding schools in Switzerland. She tied the knot too young, only to be trapped in a loveless marriage. She was rescued by some prince far handsomer than Ken. Her prince was Lars, a foreign playboy, and the heir to a toilet-paper fortune. Ken was nothing compared to Lars. Ken had reoccurring bad hair. He wore leather pants. What kind of heterosexual man wears leather pants? When Barbie had her first nervous breakdown, after she had her first baby, Lars left her. But even before that he ran around on her, crashed her cars, and spent her money. Then, when we thought it couldn't get any worse, he moved to South Beach and married Skipper. Because we all know men always leave for someone younger.

So, like my mother, my Barbie was a single mom. I was ten now, and my Barbie wore clothing and lived in the large pink plastic town house. She was rich and flew the Concorde with me several times. But she was the most miserable Barbie on the block. She was lonely. We stopped talking to each other. She was feeling old. She went to rehab for a problem with diet pills. She had a constant battle with her anorexia, and by the ripe old age of twenty-nine she was beaten up by the world. She was spent.

I was never together enough to handle Barbie (she was a very high-maintenance doll). And I was never loyal enough to her. I defected several times to She-Ra, Princess of Power; Cabbage Patch dolls; and babies who could talk. I just couldn't commit. Her hair got filled with knots. Her skin got dirty. I got bored. I stopped changing her clothing. I was the kind of kid who felt entitled and that everything was disposable.

And so we went our separate ways—I thought never to reconcile. By this time I was too old for dolls, so I moved on to ponies, pot, and Prada. I left my Barbies in the attic.

I ran with the wrong crowd. Grew up in every cliché of modern urban youth. I lost my friends to drug overdoses and car accidents. I lost myself in the noise of the city.

In my grandmother Bette's last days, I found redemption in her arms, I found meaning in my life through her death. I came back to the world, hesitantly at first, but eventually with a passion that had never been there before. And watching her die made me realize that I needed to know the things she took with her. I found everything I needed, all the secrets of my desolate childhood, in the brownstone where I grew up.

I'm not sure how I found Barbie again. It might have been when I was looking for a shawl to wear. It was the day of the funeral, and the temperature had dropped suddenly. I was cautious because the steps to the attic seemed shaky. It had been several years since I had ascended them. I pulled the chain on the single lightbulb. I looked everywhere for the shawl. I stumbled across a big brown box marked TRASH. And there she was. I pressed my forehead to hers, her soft, small, perfect, surgically enhanced nose, her flat, painted eyes, and her white-blond hair. She was as she had been at one time, my perfect dream.

She had been through plastic surgery, through the birth of a child, through the husband who left, through the family that had fallen apart. She had lived anorexia and addiction. She had survived. My Barbie was different, unlike the other girls'. It was through her uniqueness that she was able to survive. My whole life I had wanted to be a Mindy, and Barbie taught me that I didn't need to be. My Barbie looked perfect, but her life fell in like everyone else's. She had taught me survival in a way no one else could have. My Barbie had made it through, giving me the hope that I could, too.

Twelve Dancing Barbies

Erica Jong

Dear Molly,

Since I was a girl in the pre-Barbie age, I had no idea that you were hanging your Barbies upside down from your Tonka truck. The mother is always the last to know.

Of course, I saw that your Barbies were naked, that their clothes were lost, that they had smudges across their faces, but how could I read your history in your Barbies? I was too busy making sense of my own.

I had a dollhouse whose family consisted of a mother, a grandmother, and six children. There was a father somewhere, but he was like a tourist. He came home occasionally. The rest of the time, the family was on its own.

I identified with the mother who settled disputes among the children and fed everyone. The father was a shadowy figure who seemed, like my own father, to always be in Japan or other exotic places. The Japanese geisha dolls he brought home were never allowed in the dollhouse. They were for display only. Their feet were fixed on lacquered platforms. Their lacquered hair was

hung with silk cherry blossoms and silver-spangled hair orna-
ments. They were frozen in a stylized dance.

The dollhouse was the opposite: noisy, chaotic, full of con-
tention. No wonder Daddy left.

So I didn't buy you Barbies because I had some sort of childhood nostalgia for them. I bought them because they were *there.*

Before I had you, I imagined I would only let you play with
utopian toys. After you were born, I capitulated to consumerist
trash. Barbies were there on the shelf, Barbies were bought. I
didn't approve of them. I didn't approve of their tiny feet, strain-
ing upward to be forever ready for high heels, but I bought them
anyway. I was defeated by the lack of choice in the toy store.

Anyway, one thing I remembered from my childhood is how
children never want to be different. Give them tofu for lunch
and they trade for peanut butter and jelly. Deny them Barbies
and Barbies become the most seductive toys on Earth. When
you have a child, you have a hostage to all the trashiness of your
culture. You can no longer isolate yourself. You are part of the
common herd.

But whether you give children cornhusks or nutcrackers or
Barbies to play with, the subversive imagination of childhood
will triumph. A toy is a repository of fantasy.

I bought you Barbies because I didn't want you to feel deprived. You played with your Barbies in a way that told me I had
no say in the matter.

I have always felt that childhood requires more benign ne-
glect than it usually gets. In the favorite books of our childhood—*Mary Poppins, Winnie-the-Pooh, Alice in Wonderland*—all the
magic happens when the adults aren't looking. In fact, the adults
have to be banished for the childhood magic to occur. Alice can
only travel to Wonderland alone.

My favorite fairy tale when I was small was one called "The
Twelve Dancing Princesses." In it, twelve daughters of the king
leave their beds and travel to an underground realm of jeweled
trees where they dance all night with twelve princes. Their get-
aways would never be discovered but for the worn shoe leather

under their beds in the morning. This is a familiar pattern in fairy tales. Some mundane object transmuted in the world of fairy gives away the travelers' escape from reality. In one of the Mary Poppins stories, the Banks children forget their scarf in the magic world within the Royal Doulton plate on the mantel—and there it remains under the glaze to remind them that the land of fairy is as real as the mundane world of the nursery.

We seem to need to believe in this alternate world where wishes come true, youthful rebellion is indulged, and we cast off the shackles of our daily lives.

Why are all the Barbies naked? Because they have left the clothes in fairyland for the elves to wear. They have bartered their gorgeous finery for a few hours in a dreamland and they are never cold because the fantasies continue to warm them.

People object that Barbie's contours are unrealistic. They have missed the point. Barbie's value is in direct proportion to her unreality. Her waist is preposterously small, her feet impossibly flexed, her fingers far too flimsy to hold anything but a flower. That is precisely the point. She is clothed in our dreams. What more covering could she need?

The truth is we need Barbie dolls for grown-ups, too. All our lives would be enriched by having a fantasy doll we could strip naked and dress in our own dreams.

Love,
Mom

*P*lenty has been written about the way girls of all ages play with Barbie. But what about boys—and there are some—who have a hankering for the leggy bombshell? Novelist Meg Wolitzer describes the distinctive ways her two young sons have devised to play with—and love—their Barbie dolls.

BARBIE AS BOY TOY

Meg Wolitzer

$\mathcal{M}$y boys are playing with Barbie again. They have spent much of the day building a hideout, talking on the walkie-talkie headphones sent to them by their aunt, and watching Scooby-Doo cartoons on TV, and now it is nighttime and Barbie has been extracted from the toy chest and brought into the fray. It wouldn't have occurred to me to buy a Barbie doll for my sons, but through a series of events too boring to recount here, one happened to find its way into our home. I never thought the doll would be of more than a passing interest to my sons, since, throughout their lives, neither has ever showed the slightest interest in dolls. They have always, however, responded to all things vehicular; the soundtrack in our household is often a low-level *Vrrrrmmm* . . . as a car is pushed along the arm of a sofa. But the day Barbie arrived in the household, my sons quickly liberated her from her plastic box, and she has remained a surprisingly popular plaything ever since.

"Barbieeeeee!" screams Charlie, who's three, as he flings the doll across the living room toward his seven-year-old brother,

Gabriel. Gabriel reaches out and neatly catches the doll in one hand. As I head across the living room, the doll whizzes back toward my younger son like a well-dressed missile. If I was the mother of girls, I might fear that the presence of a Barbie doll in their lives was sending them subliminal antifeminist messages about women. I would have to work hard to teach them that looks aren't everything, and try to get them to give the doll interests beyond dressing up in front of a vanity mirror in order to entice the male doll in her life.

My own mother worried about such matters back in the late sixties and early seventies, and when my sister and I requested a Barbie doll, the request was denied. My mother never came right out and said that she disapproved of Barbie on political grounds; actually, I don't think she'd ever really given it that much thought. But I feel that she had an innate sense of Barbie as being somehow illicit, an object that should be kept out of our home if at all possible. A compromise eventually was reached; my sister and I were never given an actual Barbie doll, but were instead given Barbie's younger sister, Skipper: a less-threatening, presexual version of Barbie. Whether my mother's precautions had any tangible effect can't be known, although I do remain a strong feminist with little interest in "accessories," and my sister is a lesbian.

But as far as my two boys go, I don't need to worry unduly about the political "message" aspect of Barbie, because, for the most part, neither of my sons dwells on her anatomy or wardrobe or vacuous, made-up face. (Although I have to say that just the other day, Charlie did peer under Barbie's blouse and, noticing her two nipple-free swells, commented admiringly, "She's got big muscles!") No, for them Barbie is merely another *thing* to be played with, manipulated, occasionally talked to, but mostly flung. Barbie is highly throwable, and highly catchable, too, what with that ample head of hair. I needn't worry that my boys are learning to be disrespectful of women through their behavior toward this doll. In truth, she has never actually been humanized by them.

I have a friend whose little boy was given a baby doll when he was eighteen months old. At first he ignored her, but finally, when he saw that her eyes opened and closed, he became interested. From then on, he would move the doll repeatedly up and down so he could see this mechanical phenomenon in action. When someone asked him what his doll's name was, he proudly said, "Eye."

Dolls as machines; dolls as projectiles. Why is it that most boys don't simply sit down and dress and feed and pamper and talk to dolls? Why is it that most boys don't even *like* dolls? Back in the 1970s, *Free to Be You and Me* was a popular TV special devoted to promoting nonsexist attitudes in children. One of the song-stories was about a little boy who, to his parents' chagrin, craves a doll. His mother and father buy him a baseball and bat to try and distract him, but these gifts don't do the trick. One day, his grandmother arrives bearing a coveted, verboten doll. While William's parents begin to freak out, his grandmother explains that a doll is a wonderful present for a boy because it will teach him how to be a loving father someday.

Before I had children of my own, this story used to move me; if I had a boy someday, I swore, I would definitely let him have a doll. I would be the kind of nonsexist parent who allowed my son to express himself freely. He could have a doll—oh, what the hell, he could have an entire, well-equipped Dream House! But I never imagined that I would one day have two boys who enjoyed dolls only insofar as they could serve as rough-and-tumble objects.

Which isn't to say that my sons aren't loving and tender; they certainly are. They are kind to other children, and surprisingly sensitive to people's feelings. But these qualities don't always overtly appear in the actual *ways* in which they play. I've watched a mother in my son's preschool sit discreetly to the side of the room and beam as her daughter took care of a "sick" doll. "Oh, poor thing, you're burning hot!" the girl said, and she stuck a pretend digital thermometer in the doll's ear and announced that her fever was quite high. Liquid Tylenol was dispensed, as were a series of kisses and hugs, and the doll was tucked into bed and sung an entire medley of lullabies. It was gratifying for that mother to see the way in which her daughter used that doll as a vessel for empathy, for burgeoning maternal feelings. The little girl had clearly been treated similarly, and the results of good mothering were evident.

But what about boys, my own and others? What can be said about who they are from the way in which they go *Vrmmmm, vrmmm,* or scrutinize the moving parts of a toy, or toss a Barbie doll around a room? The truth is that I beam, too, when I watch my sons deeply involved in their play. I see how free they are in the world, how comfortable they are taking an object and creating an entire imagined universe for it. And if Barbie's tiny rosebud mouth could ever speak, I'm certain she would say she has a lot more fun with Gabriel and Charlie than she ever did with Ken.

NOTES AND REFERENCES

WHO'S THAT GIRL? THE WORLD
OF BARBIE DECONSTRUCTED

References

Anderson, Ross. "For the Love of Barbie." *Spy*, September/October 1994, pp. 40–47.

Aries, Philippe. *Centuries of Childhood*. New York: Knopf, 1962.

Ballen, Kate. "Way to Go, Ken!" *Fortune*, August 27, 1990, p. 14.

"Banned—But Not in Boston." *Newsweek*, April 24, 1995, p. 6.

Benjamin, Walter. "Unpacking My Library: A Talk About Book Collecting." In *Illuminations*, ed. Hannah Arendt. New York: Schocken Books, 1969 (1931), pp. 59–67.

Faludi, Susan. *Backlash: The Undeclared War Against American Women.* New York: Crown, 1991

Firestone, David. "While Barbie Talks Tough, G.I. Joe Goes Shopping." *The New York Times*, December 31, 1993, p. A12.

Friedan, Betty. *The Feminine Mystique*. New York: Dell, 1962

Garber, Marjorie. *Vested Interests: Cross-Dressing and Cultural Anxiety.* New York: Routledge, 1992.

Geertz, Clifford. "Deep Play: Notes on the Balinese Cockfight." In Clifford Geertz, *The Interpretation of Cultures.* New York: Basic Books, 1973, pp. 412–53.

Green, Richard. *The "Sissy Boy Syndrome" and the Development of Homosexuality.* New Haven, Conn.: Yale University Press, 1987.

Handler, Ruth, with Jacqueline Shannon. *Dream Doll: The Ruth Handler Story.* Stamford, Conn.: Longmeadow Press, 1994.

Homes, A. M. "A Real Doll." In *Mondo Barbie: An Anthology of Fiction and Poetry,* ed. Richard Peabody and Lucinda Ebersole. New York: St. Martin's Press, 1993 (1990), pp. 2–20.

Jenny Jones Show, The. Transcript of show broadcast July 5, 1993.

Jerry Springer Show, The. Transcript of show broadcast August 20, 1993.

Kingsolver, Barbara. *Pigs in Heaven.* New York: HarperPerennial, 1993.

Kraft, Ronald Mark. "Open Quote." *Genre,* November 1994, p. 14.

Land-Weber, Ellen. *The Passionate Collector.* New York: Simon & Schuster, 1980.

Lord, M. G. *Forever Barbie: The Unauthorized Biography of a Real Doll.* New York: William Morrow, 1994.

Masciola, Carol. "Doll Heist." *Los Angeles Times,* October 14, 1992, pp. A1, 18.

Muensterberger, Werner. *Collecting: An Unruly Passion: Psychological Perspectives.* Princeton, N.J.: Princeton University Press, 1993.

Packard, Vance. *The Hidden Persuaders.* New York: D. McKay, 1957.

Pereira, Joseph. "Quick Math: Mattel's Dumb Doll Adds Up to Be a Collector's Item." *The Wall Street Journal,* December 21, 1992.

Quindlen, Anna. "Barbie at 35." *The New York Times,* September 10, 1994, p. 19.

Randolph, Eleanor. "The One and Only Barbie Goes to Russia." *Los Angeles Times,* September 3, 1992, p. E10.

"She's No Barbie, Nor Does She Care to Be." *The New York Times*, August 16, 1991, p. CII.

Signorile, Michelangelo. *Queer in America: Sex, the Media, and the Closets of Power.* New York: Anchor Books, 1993.

Smith, Lynn. "Not Only Fun, But P.C. Too," *Los Angeles Times*, October 30, 1992, pp. EI, E8.

Stewart, Doug. "In the World of Toy Sales, Child's Play Is Serious Business." *Smithsonian*, December 1989, pp. 73–83.

Taylor, John. "Mommy-to-Be Doll Raises Eyebrows, Ire." *Omaha World-Herald*, May 3, 1992, p. EI.

Thorson, Alice. "Barbie's Birthday." *Kansas City Star*, September 3, 1994, pp. EI–2.

Watanabe, Teresa. "'Doll Wars' Challenge Female Ideal." *Los Angeles Times*, October 27, 1992, p. H2.

Wolf, Naomi. *The Beauty Myth: How Images of Beauty Are Used Against Women.* New York: Anchor Books, 1992.

Yoe, Craig, ed. *The Art of Barbie: Artists Celebrate the World's Favorite Doll.* New York: Workman, 1994.

GOLDEN OLDIE:
BARBIE IN THE 1950S

Notes

1. For details of Mattel product researchers' findings that mothers hated the doll and girls loved it, see M. G. Lord, *Forever Barbie: The Unauthorized Biography of a Real Doll* (New York: William Morrow, 1994), and Tom Englehardt, *The End of Victory Culture: Cold War America and the Dissillusioning of a Generation* (New York: Basic Books, 1995), p. 148.

2. The true details from the Nelsons' lives can be seen in the documentary *Ozzie and Harriet: The Adventures of America's Favorite Family*, directed by Peter Jones for A&E. See also Bernard Weinraub, "Dousing the Glow of TV's First Family," *The New York Times*, June 18, 1998, pp. BI, B4; Caryn James, "Fairy-Tale Family's Grim Chapters," *The New York Times*, June 19, 1998. On the difficult private life of Sandra

Dee, see Dodd Darin, *The Magnificent Shattered Life of Bobby Darin and Sandra Dee* (New York: Warner Books, 1995). On the incest story of Miss America 1958, see Marilyn Van Derbur Atler, "The Darkest Secret," *People*, June 10, 1991, pp. 88–94.

3. Susan M. Hartmann, *The Home Front and Beyond: American Women in the 1940s* (Boston: Twayne Publishers, 1982), pp. 43–45; Stephanie Coontz, *The Way We Never Were: American Families and the Nostalgia Trap* (New York: Basic Books, 1992), p. 159; John D'Emilio and Estelle Freedman, *Intimate Matters: A History of Sexuality in America* (New York: Harper and Row, 1988), pp. 260–61, 268; Sherna Berger Gluck, *Rosie the Riveter Revisited: Women, the War, and Social Change* (Boston: Twayne Publishers, 1987); Andrea Walsh, *Women's Film and Female Experience, 1940–1950* (New York: Praeger, 1984).

4. Coontz, *The Way We Never Were*, p. 160; William Chafe, *The Paradox of Change: American Women in the Twentieth Century* (New York: Oxford University Press, 1991); Andrew Cherlin, "Changing Family and Household: Contemporary Lessons from Historical Research," *American Review of Sociology* 9 (1983): 59.

5. Susan Ware, "American Women in the 1950s: Nonpartisan Politics and Women's Politicization," in *Women, Politics, and Change*, ed. Louise Tilly and Patricia Gurin (New York: Russell Sage, 1990), pp. 281–99; Elaine Tyler May, *Homeward Bound: American Families in the Cold War Era* (New York: Basic Books, 1988); Susan Hartman, "Women's Employment and the Domestic Ideal in the Early Cold War Years," in *Not June Cleaver: Women and Gender in Postwar America, 1945–60*, ed. Joanne Meyerowitz (Philadelphia: Temple University Press, 1994), pp. 84–100; Joanne Meyerowitz, "Beyond the Feminine Mystique: A Reassessment of the Postwar Mass Culture, 1946–1958," in Meyerowitz, *Not June Cleaver*, pp. 229–62.

6. Quoted in Wini Breines, "The 1950s: Gender and Some Social Science," *Sociological Inquiry* 56 (1986): 77–78.

7. On mother blaming, see Marynia Farnham and Ferdinand Lundberg, *Modern Women: The Lost Sex* (New York: Grosset and Dunlap, 1947), and Molly Ladd-Tayler and Lauri Umanski, *"Bad" Mothers: The Politics of Blame in Twentieth-Century America*. Interview quoted in Jessica Weiss, "Rethinking the Baby Boom on Postwar Family Life," paper presented at the Pacific Coast Branch of the American Historical Association, August 1993, p. 9.

8. Ilene Philipson, "Heterosexual Antagonisms and the Politics of Mothering," *Socialist Review* 66 (1982): vol. 99, pp. 55–77.

9. Wini Breines, "The 'Other' Fifties: Beats and Bad Girls," in Meyerowitz, *Not June Cleaver*, pp. 382–407.

10. The quotes and evaluation of Parson's analysis in this paragraph come from Brines, "The 1950s: Gender and Some Social Science," pp. 78–79.

11. Marjorie Rosen, *Popcorn Venus: Women, Movies, and the American Dream* (New York: Avon Books, 1973), p. 309; Stephanie Coontz, *The Way We Really Are: Coming to Terms with America's Changing Families* (New York: Basic Books, 1997), p. 40; D'Emilio and Freedman, *Intimate Matters*, pp. 264, 249.

12. Advertising quote cited in Coontz, *The Way We Never Were*, p. 171. For an extended discussion of the containment strategy and its holes, see May, *Homeward Bound*.

13. Quoted in Coontz, *The Way We Never Were*, p. 171.

14. The Dichter strategy is described in Lord, *Forever Barbie*, pp. 40–41.

15. Coontz, *The Way We Really Are*, p. 44.

Notes

1. M. G. Lord, *Forever Barbie: The Unauthorized Biography of a Real Doll* (New York: William Morrow, 1994), p. 6.

2. Jacqueline Urla and Alan C. Swedlund, "The Anthropometry of Barbie: Unsettling Ideals of the Feminine Body in Popular Culture," in *Deviant Bodies: Critical Perspectives on Difference in Science and Popular Culture,* ed. Jennifer Terry and Jacqueline Urla (Bloomington: Indiana University Press, 1995), p. 302; and Erica Rand, *Barbie's Queer Accessories* (Durham, N.C.: Duke University Press, 1995), p. 9.

3. Urla and Swedlund, "The Anthropometry of Barbie," pp. 297–98.

4. Lord, *Forever Barbie,* p. 213.

5. Rand, *Barbie's Queer Accessories,* pp. 44–45.

6. Cynthia Robins, *Barbie: Thirty Years of America's Doll* (New York: Contemporary Books, 1989), p. 32.

7. Carroll cited in Robins, *Barbie,* p. 49.

8. Roland Barthes cited in Linda Nochlin, "The Imaginary Orient." In Linda Nochlin, *The Politics of Vision: Essays on Nineteenth-Century Art and Society* (New York: Harper and Row, 1989), p. 38.

9. Robins, *Barbie,* p. 71.

10. Ibid., *Barbie,* p. 121.

11. Urla and Swedlund, "The Anthropometry of Barbie," p. 282.

12. Ibid. p. 301.

13. Ibid.

14. Lord, *Forever Barbie,* p. 274.

References

Billy Boy. *Barbie: Her Life and Times.* New York: Crown, 1987.

"The Barbie Chronicles" (photographs). Brown, Dean. http://www.erols.com/browndk/.

"Liposuction Barbie." http://www.mit.edu:8001/activities/ is764/ barbie.html.

Clark, Kenneth. *The Nude: A Study in Ideal Form.* Princeton, N.J.: Princeton: University Press, 1956.

duCille, Ann. "Dyes and Dolls: Multicultural Barbie and the Merchandising of Difference." *Differences: A Journal of Feminist Cultural Studies* 6 (1994): 1.

Lord, M. G. *Forever Barbie: The Unauthorized Biography of a Real Doll.* New York: William Morrow, 1994.

Nochlin, Linda. "The Imaginary Orient." In Linda Nochlin, *The Politics of Vision: Essays on Nineteenth-Century Art and Society.* New York: Harper and Row, 1989.

Rand, Erica. *Barbie's Queer Accessories.* Durham, N.C.: Duke University Press, 1995.

Robins, Cynthia. *Barbie: Thirty Years of America's Doll.* New York: Contemporary Books, 1989.

Urla, Jacqueline, and Alan C. Swedlund. "The Anthropometry of Barbie: Unsettling Ideals of the Feminine Body in Popular Culture." In *Deviant Bodies: Critical Perspectives on Difference in Science and Popular Culture,* ed. Jennifer Terry and Jacqueline Urla. Bloomington: Indiana University Press, 1995.

Vamos, Igor (director, producer, editor). "BLO 'Operation Newspeak' 1993–94."

BARBIE'S BODY PROJECT

Notes

1. See, for instance, the following articles: On Barbie and negative body image, Anna Quindlen, "Barbie at 35," *The New York Times,* September 10, 1994, p. 19 [reprinted in this collection]; on race, body image, and commodification, Ann

duCille, "Toy Theory," in *Skin Trade* (Cambridge, Mass.: Harvard University Press, 1996), pp. 9–59; on consumerism, Marilyn Ferris Motz, "I Want to Be a Barbie Doll When I Grow Up: The Cultural Significance of Barbie Doll," *The Popular Culture Reader*, ed. Christopher D. Geist and Jack Nachbar (Bowling Green State: Bowling Green, Ohio University Popular Press, 1983), pp. 122–35. For a positive assessment of Barbie, see Yona Zeldis McDonough, "What Barbie Really Taught Me: Lessons from the Playrooms, Both Naughty and Nice," *The New York Times,* January 25, 1995, p. 70. [A longer version of this article appears in this collection.]

2. Joan Jacobs Brumberg, *The Body Project* (New York: Random House, 1997), p. xvii.

3. Ibid., p. xx.

4. Ibid., p. 11.

5. Ibid., p. 18.

6. I won't try the patience of my readers by listing every available product, but I give a representative sampling. The typicality of these in-stock items were confirmed by trips to other variety stores with Barbie aisles, such as Hills and Big Kmart in Ithaca, New York.

7. In an information package for consumers, Mattel lists these dolls in a different category and on a different page from the other Barbie dolls. Their age designation is also different. For instance, the Lucille Ball as Lucy Ricardo doll is recommended for age fourteen and over, while Bead Blast Barbie is recommended for age three and over. However, some of the special-edition dolls cross categories, such as Rapunzel Barbie, whose hair can be let down again and again, and who is stocked in the aisle with the children's Barbies.

8. Wedding and birthday dolls and outfits have been issued regularly, especially in recent years. Since 1990, Mattel has

manufactured a birthday doll every year. This is remarkable because, as Mattel notes in "Barbie: Frequently Asked Questions," an informational release, "themes are replaced almost every year." By 1991, Mattel had sold more wedding dresses than any other costume. See Beverly Beyette, "A Dress-Up Job: Barbie's Principal Designer Scales Down Glamour and Plays Up Fantasy," *Los Angeles Times*, February 6, 1991, p. E5, cited by Erica Rand in *Barbie's Queer Accessories* (Durham, N.C.: Duke University Press, 1995). I am indebted to this excellent book for much of my knowledge of Barbie history. Mattel manufactured wedding dolls in 1990, 1991, and 1996.

9. Since 1980, Mattel had produced three Barbies who participate in traditionally unglamorous male sports: WNBA Basketball Barbie, NBA Commemorative Barbie (actually a series of dolls who wear uniforms of various popular teams), and a Barbie who plays soccer (soon to be available).

10. The name of Lily fashion line (and of its owner, Ms. Lily) is an insider's joke on Barbie's origins. Barbie was modeled after a German doll named Lilli, produced in the mid-1950s. See Rand, *Barbie's Queer Accessories*, pp. 32–38. See also Billy Boy, *Barbie: Her Life and Times* (New York: Crown, 1987), p. 19.

11. Barbara Slate, *Very Busy Barbie* (Racine, Wisc.: Golden Books, 1993). The book does not have page numbers. The quotations are taken, respectively, from the last two pages of the book.

12. Most Barbie books today are published by Golden Books, reflecting the declining age of girls who play with Barbie. Barbie books of the sixties tended to be young-adult novels, which centered around Barbie's romances. See Rand, *Barbie's Queer Accessories*, pp. 48–58 and *passim*. Because of their official sponsorship, critics tend to discuss these

books as homogeneous. However, I have noticed an important distinction between the Grolier Barbie books (available through the Barbie book club) and others. These books, directed at a somewhat older audience than the Golden Books, represent a Barbie whose life does not center around glamour and body projects. In the four introductory books I received for joining the club, Barbie is a model in only one. In two of the others, she is, respectively, a teacher and a tourist on an archaeological dig (who dreams she is an Egyptian princess). The fourth does not mention a career.

13. Nancy Parent, *Barbie's Special Night* (Burbank, Calif.: Fun Works, 1996). I cite the last page.

14. In "Barbie: Frequently Asked Questions," Mattel finesses the issue of Barbie's age: "How old is Barbie doll? Barbie made her debut at the American Toy Fair, New York, February 1959."

15. Rand, *Barbie's Queer Accessories*, p. 40.

16. Ibid., p. 53.

17. Ibid., p. 90.

18. "Barbie: Frequently Asked Questions:" treats the issue of Barbie's family as follows: "Barbie doll has sisters and brothers; yet she does not have parents. Why? Actually, Barbie doll has parents, but Mattel has never manufactured them. Their names are George and Margaret Roberts."

19. Rita Balducci, *Girl's Best Friend* (Danbury, Conn.: Grolier Enterprises, 1998).

20. Bonnie Lasser, *Let's Have a Sleepover* (New York: Golden Books, 1998).

21. Marie Morreale, *In the Spotlight* (New York: Golden Books, 1998).

22. Two Doll House sets feature dressing up for the little-girl figures: the Dream Wardrobe—Lots of Clothes for Dress-

Up Fun and the Dress-Up Vanity Set. But these sets are more about emulating the adults in the house, as children have done from time immemorial, than about adorning the body. The sets include furniture for the Doll House, which suggests that the children are trying on either costumes or their parents' clothing. The set lacks the conjuncture of adornment, isolation, and consumerism that we see in the Dress Shop.

23. See note I.

24. "Barbie reception" is the subject of *Barbie's Queer Accessories*. I argue here along similar lines (although much more concisely). Rand also recounts many instances of subversive Barbie play among children.

25. However, she did point out that the line of products has changed in the last twenty years, with many more items revolving around adornment for the child. She speculated that this might change the child's relationship to Barbie play. As I've tried to show, this is a disturbing development, indicative of our increased emphasis on the body in the culture at large, but whether this makes Barbie a "dangerous" toy remains to be seen. Perhaps women growing up twenty years from now will have very different feelings and memories about what it meant to have a Barbie doll.

BARBIE IN BLACK AND WHITE

Notes

I. After many calls to the Jamaican embassy in Washington and to various cultural organizations in Jamaica, I have concluded that Jamaican Barbie's costume—a floor-length granny dress with apron and headrag—bears some resemblance to what is considered the island's traditional folk costume. But it was also made clear to me that these costumes have more to do with tourism than with local traditions. According to media-relations director Donna Gibbs at Mattel, decisions about costuming are made by the design and marketing teams in consulation with other senior staffers. The attempt, Gibbs informed me, "is to determine and roughly approximate" the national costume of each country in the collection (conversation, September 9, 1994). I still wonder, though, about the politics of these design decisions: why the doll representing Jamaica is figured as a maid, while the doll representing Great Britain is presented as a lady—a blond, blue-eyed Barbie doll dressed in a fancy riding habit with boots and hat.

2. Actually, in Jamaica *patois* is spelled differently: *potwah*, I believe.

3. See, e.g., Morris Rosenberg, *Conceiving the Self* (New York: Basic Books, 1979) and *Society and the Adolescent Self-Image* (Hanover, N.H.: University Press of New England, 1989), and William E. Cross, *Shades of Black: Diversity in African American Identity* (Philadelphia: Temple University Press, 1991), which challenge the Clarks' findings. The psycholgoist Na'im Akbar argues that just as the Moynihan Report pathologized the black family, the Clark doll studies pathologized the black community by the implied assumption that it was "psychologically unhealthy for 'colored' children to go to school only with one another," since "the outcome is likely to be self-hatred, lowered motivation, and so on." According to Akbar, this problematic assumption gave rise to a racist logical fallacy embedded in the 1954 Supreme Court decision: that it was "psychologically healthy for Black children to attend school with white children," since "such an opportunity is likely to improve the African-American child's self-concept, intellectual achievement, and overall social and psychological adjustment." See No'im Akbar, "Our Destiny: Authors of a Scientific Revolution," in *Black Children: Social, Educational, and Parental Environments*, ed. Harriette Pipes McAdoo and John Lewis McAdoo (Beverly Hills, Calif.: Sage Publications, 1985),

pp. 24–25. Akbar's analysis seems to miss the point that what concerned black parents in the 1950s (as well as before and since) was the material effects of Jim Crow education: separate was not equal.

4. Harriette Pipes McAdoo, "Racial Attitudes and Self Concept of Young Black Children over Time," in McAdoo and McAdoo, *Black Children*, p. 214.

5. Darlene Powell Hopson and Derek S. Hopson, *Different and Wonderful: Raising Black Children in a Race-Conscious Society* (New York: Simon and Schuster, 1990), pp. xix–xx.

6. Ibid., p. 127; my emphasis. "*You do not want your child to grow up thinking that only White dolls, and by extension White people, are attractive and nice,*" the Hopsons go on to explain (emphasis in the original).

7. The cover of the November/December 1993 issue of *Barbie* offers a good illustration of my point. It is dominated by a full-page image of white Happy Holiday Barbie. Tucked away in a tiny insert in the upper-left corner is the face of a black Barbie doll, presumably stuck in to let us know that Happy Holiday Barbie also comes in black. Black Barbie was the cover story in *Barbie Bazaar,* May/June 1996.

8. Hopson and Hopson, *Different and Wonderful,* pp. 119, 124.

9. It is also clear that other factors influenced Mattel's decision to go ethnic, including a marketing survey done in the late 1980s that reportedly identified the top fourteen cities with the highest concentrations of black residents. According to the doll dealer and appraiser A. Glenn Mandeville, Mattel used this information and the complaints and suggestions of consumers to help develop its Shani line. In his words, "Mattel has indeed gone out in the 1990s to make sure they capture all markets." *Doll Fashion Anthology and Price Guide,* 3rd ed. (Cresaptown, Md.: Hobby House Press, 1992), p. 174.

10. Asha is a variant of the Swahili and Arabic name Aisha or Ayisha, meaning "life" or "alive." It is also the name of Mohammed's chief wife. As a minor point of interest, Nichelle is the first name of the black actress (Nichelle Nichols) who played Lieutenant Uhura on the original *Star Trek* TV series (1966–69).

11. Quoted in Lisa Jones, "A Doll is Born," *Village Voice,* March 26, 1991, p. 36.

12. Kenyan Barbie, introduced in 1994, has the most closely cropped hair of any Barbie doll to date. I asked Donna Gibbs if Mattel was concerned that the doll's severely cropped hair (little more than peach fuzz, or what a colleague described as "Afro turf") would hamper sales. She told me that the company expected Kenyan Barbie to sell as well as all the other national dolls, which are intended more for adult collectors. Kenyan Barbie received a "short-cropped Afro in an attempt to make her look more authentic," Gibbs informed me. "She represents a more authentic-looking doll." (The doll also has bare feet and wears Mattel's interpretation of the native dress of the Masai woman; the first-person narrative on the back of the box tells us that most Kenyan people wear modern dress and that spears are banned in the city.)

13. Gibbs, conversation, September 9, 1994.

14. See Gerald Early, "Life with Daughters: Watching the Miss America Pageant," in his *The Culture of Bruising: Essays on Prizefighting, Literature, and Modern American Culture* (Hopewell, N.J.: Ecco Press, 1994), p. 268.

15. Among many texts on the politics of black people's hair, see Cheryl Clarke's poem "Hair: A Narrative," in her *Narratives: Poems in the Tradition of Black Women* (New York: Kitchen Table/Women of Color Press, 1982); Kobena Mercer, "Black Hair/Style Politics," in Russell Ferguson, Martha Gever, Trinh T. Minh-ha, and Cornell West, eds., *Out There:*

Marginalization and Contemporary Cultures (New York and Cambridge, Mass.: New Museum of Contemporary Art and MIT Press, 1992), pp. 247–64; and Ayoka Chinzera, director, *Hairpiece: A Film for Nappy-Headed People*, 1982. In fiction, see Toni Morrison's *The Bluest Eye*.

16. I intend no value judgment in making this observation about what we do with our hair. Though Afros, braids, and dreadlocks may be seen by some as more "authentically black" or more Afrocentrically political than straightened or chemically processed hair, I am inclined to agree with Kobena Mercer that all black hairstyles are political as a historical ethnic signifier (in "Black Hair/Style Politics," p. 251). It is history that has made black hair *"mean."*

17. Ibid., pp. 247–48.

18. Jacqueline Urla and Alan Swedlund, "The Anthropometry of Barbie: Unsettling Ideas of the Feminine in Popular Culture," in *Deviant Bodies: Critical Perspectives on Difference in Science and Popular Culture*, ed. Jennifer Terry and Jacqueline Urla (Bloomington: Indiana University Press, 1995).

19. Sander L. Gilman, "Black Bodies, White Bodies: Toward an Iconography of Female Sexuality in Late-Nineteenth-Century Art, Medicine, and Literature," in *"Race," Writing, and Difference*, ed. Henry Louis Gates Jr. (Chicago: University of Chicago Press, 1985), p. 238.

20. See Stephen Jay Gould, "The Hottentot Venus," *Natural History* 91 (1982): 20–27. For a poetic interpretation of Sarah Bartmann's story, see the title poem in Elizabeth Alexander's *The Venus Hottentot* (Charlottesville: University of Virginia Press, 1990), pp. 3–7.

21. Anne Fausto Sterling, "Gender, Race, and Nation: The Comparative Anatomy of 'Hottentot' Women in Europe: 1815–1817," in Terry and Urla, *Deviant Bodies*, pp. 19–48.

22. Gilman, "Black Bodies, White Bodies," p. 232.

Notes

1. Other studies of dolls include Allyson Booth, "Battered Dolls," in *Images of the Child*, ed. Harry Eiss (Bowling Green, Ohio.: Bowling Green State University Popular Press, 1994), pp. 143–52; and Kathy Merlock Jackson, "Targeting Baby-Boom Children as Consumers: Mattel Uses Television to Sell Talking Dolls," in Eiss, *Images of the Child*, pp. 187–97.

2. Additional recent studies in girls' culture include Sally Mitchell, *The New Girl: Girls' Culture in England, 1880–1915* (New York: Columbia University Press, 1995); Lynne Vallone, *Discipline of Virtue: Girls' Culture in the Eighteenth and Nineteenth Centuries* (New Haven, Conn.: Yale University Press, 1995); and Lynne Vallone and Claudia Nelson, eds., *The Girl's Own: Cultural Histories of the Anglo-American Girl, 1830–1915* (Athens: University of Georgia Press, 1994). Also, see my *Delinquents and Debutantes: Twentieth-Century American Girls' Culture* (New York: New York University Press, 1998); *Intimate Communities: Representation and Social Transformation in Women's College Fiction, 1895–1910* (Bowling Green, Ohio: Bowling Green State University Popular Press, 1995); *Millennium Girls: Today's Girls Around the World* (Lanham, Md.: Rowman and Littlefield, 1998); and *Nancy Drew and Company: Culture, Gender, and Girls' Series* (Bowling Green, Ohio: Bowling Green State University Popular Press, 1997).

3. Miriam Formanek-Brunell, *Made to Play House: Dolls and the Commercialization of American Girlhood, 1830–1930* (New Haven, Conn.: Yale University Press, 1993), p. 1.

4. Roland Barthes, *Mythologies* (New York: Hill and Wang, 1986 [1957]), p. 53.

CONTRIBUTORS

JEANNE MARIE BEAUMONT is the author of *Placebo Effects* (W. W. Norton, 1997). She is coeditor of *American Letters & Commentary,* and teaches writing at Rutgers University in New Brunswick, New Jersey.

PAMELA BRANDT is the author of a novel, *Becoming the Butlers* (Bantam, 1990). Her fiction and poetry have appeared in *The Pushcart Prize Anthology: The Best of the Small Presses,* as well as *The Edinburgh Review, The Ontario Review, Real Fiction,* and other magazines. She teaches English at the Chapin School in New York City. Her daughter, Natalie, age six, currently owns eleven Barbie dolls.

STEPHANIE COONTZ teaches history and family studies at Evergreen State College in Olympia, Washington. Recent books include *The Way We Never Were: American Families and the Nostalgia Trap* (Basic Books, 1992) and *The Way We Really Are: Coming to Terms with America's Changing Families* (Basic Books, 1997). She also edited, with Maya Parson and Gabrielle Raley, *American Families: A Multicultural Reader* (Routledge, 1999).

STEVEN C. DUBIN received his Ph.D. in 1982 and his first Barbie a dozen years later. He directs the Media, Society, and the Arts Program at Purchase College—State University of New York, and has written extensively about art and artists, popular culture, censorship, and the culture wars. His books include *Bureaucratizing the Muse* (University of Chicago Press, 1987); *Arresting Images* (Routledge, 1992), which was cited by *The New York Times* as a Notable Book of the Year in 1992 and by the Gustavus Myers Center for the Study of Human Rights as an Outstanding Book of 1993; and *Displays of Power* (New York University Press, 1999). He has compensated for his late entry into the world of Barbie by acquiring more of the dolls than he cares to admit to publicly.

ANN DUCILLE is a professor of American and African-American literature at the University of California, San Diego. She received a Guggenheim Fellowship in 1994 and is the author of *The Coupling Convention: Sex, Text and Tradition in Black Women's Fiction* (Oxford University Press, 1993) and *Skin Trade* (Harvard University Press, 1996).

DENISE DUHAMEL is the author of ten books and chapbooks of poetry. Her most recent titles are *The Star-Spangled Banner* (Southern Illinois University Press, 1999), winner of the Crab Orchard Poetry Prize; *Exquisite Politics*, a collaborative work with Maureen Seaton (Tia Chucha Press, 1997); *Kinky* (Orchises Press, 1997), *Girl Soldier* (Garden Street Press, 1996), and *How the Sky Fell*, which won the Pearl Editions chapbook contest in 1996. She has been anthologized widely, including in three editions of Scribner's *The Best American Poetry* (1993, 1994, and 1998).

MELISSA HOOK is a writer whose work has appeared in *Parabola, Tricycle: The Buddhist Review,* and *Publishers Weekly*. She lives in New York City and south-central Pennsylvania. Some of her happiest moments are spent working on her solar-powered house on a Mediterranean island off the coast of southern Spain.

SHERRIE A. INNESS is an associate professor of English at Miami University. She is the author of *Intimate Communities: Representatives and Social Transformation in Women's College Fiction, 1895–1910* (Bowling Green, 1995), and *Tough Girls: Women Warriors and Wonder Women in Popular Culture* (University of Pennsylvania Press, 1999). She is also the editor of *Nancy Drew and Company: Culture, Gender, and Girls' Series* (Bowling Green, 1997), *Delinquents and Debutantes: Twentieth-Century American Girls' Cultures* (New York University Press, 1998) and *Millennium Girls: Today's Girls Around the World* (Rowman & Littlefield, 1998).

WENDY SINGER JONES has taught at the University of Rochester, Williams College, and Cornell University since receiving her Ph.D. in English from Cornell. She is the author of articles and books on eighteenth- and nineteenth-century fiction, and is currently working on a book about feminism in the English novel. She lives in Ithaca, New York, with her husband and two daughters.

ERICA JONG, poet, novelist, and essayist, is best known for her six bestselling novels, including *Fear of Flying* (Holt, Rinehart & Winston, 1973), and six award-winning collections of poetry. Her work has been translated into twenty-seven languages. Known for her commitment to women's rights, authors' rights, and free expression, Ms. Jong is a frequent lecturer in the United States and abroad. Ms. Jong's latest book, *What Do Women Want?* was published by HarperCollins in 1998.

MOLLY JONG-FAST was born in 1978 and grew up in New York City. Molly is a freelance journalist and sometime humor essayist. She is working on a novel for Villard which is due out in the United States in spring 2000, with a simultaneous publication by Hoddard and Strough in England. She is the daughter of Erica Jong and the granddaughter of Howard Fast.

M. G. LORD is the author of *Forever Barbie: The Unauthorized Life of a Real Doll* (William Morrow, 1994). Her work has appeared in *The New York Times, The Washington Post, The New Yorker, Vogue, Vanity Fair, Lingua Franca,* and *Newsday,* where for over a decade she was on staff as a columnist and political cartoonist. She currently lives in Los Angeles and is working on an informal cultural history of NASA's Jet Propulsion Laboratory for Simon & Schuster.

YONA ZELDIS MCDONOUGH's articles and fiction have appeared in many national magazines and literary reviews. She is also the author of several children's books, including *Anne Frank* (Henry Holt, 1997) and *Sisters in Strength: American Women Who Made a Difference* (Henry Holt, 2000). She lives in Brooklyn, New York, with her husband and two children.

CAROL OCKMAN is Professor of Art History at Williams College and author of *Ingres's Eroticized Bodies: Retracing the Serpentine Line* (Yale University Press, 1995). She is currently at work on a book about Sarah Bernhardt and mass culture entitled *"Who Do You Think You Are, Sarah Bernhardt?"* Ockman lectures on the culture of nineteenth-century France and our own fin de siècle, reviews contemporary art for *Artforum,* and is consultant and contributor to the Bernhardt exhibition scheduled for the year 2002 at The Jewish Museum New York. She was a fellow at the Bunting Institute at Radcliffe College 1997–98.

LESLIE PARIS is a doctoral candidate in American culture at the University of Michigan. Her research focuses on the cultural history of gender, recreation, and childhood in the twentieth century. She is currently completing a dissertation about New York children at summer camps in the interwar years.

ANNA QUINDLEN is the author of three bestselling novels, *Object Lessons* (Random House, 1991), *One True Thing* (Random House, 1994), and *Black and Blue* (Random House, 1998). Her *New York Times* column "Public and Private" won a Pulitzer Prize in 1992, and a selection of these columns was published as *Thinking Out Loud* (Fawcett Books, 1994). A collection of her "Life in the 30s" columns was published as *Living Out Loud* (Fawcett, 1994). She is also the author of two children's books.

SUSAN SCHNUR is a rabbi whose paper pulpit is *Lilith* magazine, the Jewish-feminist quarterly published in New York City. She is also a clinical psychologist at Princeton University.

SUSAN SHAPIRO, freelance humor writer, is the author of *Male-to-Female Dictionary* (Berkley/Comedy Central, 1996) and *Internal Medicine* (IM Press, 1997). She teaches writing at New York University and the New School.

CAROL SHIELDS is a novelist and playwright. In 1995 she won the Pulitzer Prize for fiction for her novel *The Stone Diaries* (Viking Press). Her most recent novel is *Larry's Party* (Viking Press, 1997), which was awarded Britain's Orange Prize. She is a professor of English at the University of Manitoba and Chancellor of the University of Winnipeg.

JANE SMILEY was born in Los Angeles, grew up in St. Louis, and studied at Vassar and the University of Iowa, where she received her Ph.D. She is the author of nine works of fiction, including *The Age of Grief* (Knopf, 1987), *The Greenlanders* (Knopf, 1988), *Ordinary Love and Good Will* (Knopf, 1989), *A Thousand Acres* (Knopf, 1991)—winner of Pulitzer Prize, the National Book Critics Circle Award, and the Chicago Tribune Heartland Prize—*Moo* (Knopf, 1995), and *The All-True Travels and Adventures of Lidie Newton* (Knopf, 1998). She currently lives in Northern California.

MARIFLO STEPHENS writes essays and fiction from the home she shares with her husband and two daughters in Charlottesville, Virginia. Her work has been published in numerous periodicals, including *The Washington Post* and the *Virginia Quarterly Review*. "Barbie Doesn't Live Here Anymore" is part of her memoir-in-progress, *Last One Home: Life After Oprah*.

DAVID TRINIDAD's books include *Answer Song* (High Risk Books, 1994) and *Hand Over Heart: Poems 1981–1988* (Serpent's Tail, 1991). He currently teaches poetry at Rutgers University, where he directs the Writers at Rutgers series, and is a member of the core faculty in the M.F.A. writing program at the New School for Social Research. His book *Plasticville* will be published by Turtle Point Press in 2000. Originally from Los Angeles, Trinidad has lived in New York City since 1988.

MEG WOLITZER's most recent novel is *Surrender, Dorothy* (Scribner, 1999). Her fiction has appeared in *The Best American Short Stories 1998* and *The Pushcart Prize Anthology: The Best of the Small Presses, 1999*. She lives in New York City.

INDEX

Note: Page numbers followed by *n* indicate material in numbered endnotes.